Learning Together as God's Royal Family

Learning Together as God's Royal Family

Keswick 2002

Edited by Ali Hull

Authentic
LIFESTYLE

Copyright © The Keswick Convention Council 2002

First Published in 2002 by Authentic Lifestyle

08 07 06 05 04 03 02   7 6 5 4 3 2 1

Authentic Lifestyle is an imprint of Authentic Media,
PO Box 300, Carlisle, Cumbria CA3 0QS, UK
And PO Box 1047, Waynesboro, GA 30830-2047, USA
www.paternoster-publishing.com

British Library Cataloguing in Publication Data

A catalogue record for this book is available from
the British Library

ISBN 1-85078-471-X

Unless otherwise stated, Scripture quotations are taken from the
HOLY BIBLE, NEW INTERNATIONAL VERSION
Copyright © 1973, 1978, 1984 by the International Bible Society.
Used by permission of Hodder and Stoughton Limited. All rights reserved.
NIV is a registered trademark of the International Bible Society
UK trademark number 1448790. Some quotations were paraphrased by the speakers
or taken from THE MESSAGE

Cover design by Diane Bainbridge
Photography © Adam Greene and Keswick Convention Council
Printed in Great Britain by
Cox and Wyman, Reading Berkshire

Contents

Introduction by the Chairman of the 2002 Convention   vii

Editor's Introduction   ix

The Bible Readings

The Greatest Story Ever Told
Studies in John 17 – 21
   by Bruce Milne   3

1   Intercession
      John 17:1-26   5
2   Confrontation
      John 18:1-40   17
3   Oblation
      John 19:1-42   31
4   Resurrection
      John 20:1-31   43
5   Mission
      John 21:1-25   57

Visions of God
Themes from Ezekiel
   by Liam Goligher   69

1   Vision Express
      Ezekiel 1:1 – 3:15   71
2   When God leaves the building
      Ezekiel 8 – 11   83
3   The Good Shepherd
      Ezekiel 34   95
4   Can these bones live?
      Ezekiel 37   107

5   A river runs through it
      Ezekiel 40 – 48   119

The Addresses

Manifesto of the King
   by Peter Lewis   135

Submission to the King
   by Victor Jack   147

Children of the King
   by Dominic Smart   159

The King is among us
   by Rico Tice   171

Submission to the King
   by Peter Maiden   183

Brought into the Kingdom
   by Liam Goligher   195

Behold your King
   by Rob Warner   207

Keswick 2002 Tapes, Videos and Books   221

Keswick 2003   223

Introduction by the Chairman of the 2002 Convention

Keswick 2002 was memorable. The crowds were memorable, on one or two occasions a few more than the tent could accommodate.

But the ministry of God's word and the response of His people was the memory that will live on. There was no absence of laughter throughout the three weeks but at the same time often a solemnity in the tent as we responded to the voice of God.

Two themes recurred throughout the Convention. The reality of eternity – we must live our lives making our value decisions in the light of eternity. We cannot keep silent – we must boldly witness when the consequences are eternal.

There were many highlights. Few present will forget Bruce Milne's exposition of John 19 as we were brought so movingly to the cross. Liam Goligher's masterly overview of Ezekiel 40 – 48 gave great confidence as we saw the purposes of God being unerringly fulfilled.

I trust you will enjoy this record of some of the Convention ministry and that it will wet your spiritual appetite so that you will be with us for the 2003 Convention.

Our theme will be discipleship which transforms all of our lives – family, work, church, leisure.

See you there unless the eternal day has dawned! Let's continue to make all our decisions in the light of that reality.

Peter Maiden, Chairman

Editor's Introduction

Editing the Keswick Year Book has once again been the highlight of my autumn, just as attending the event is the best bit about my summer. Once again, we faced the problem of how to get as much of this superb material into the book, and whether we should change the format more radically. In the end, it was decided that Steve Brady's Bible readings from week three should provide the basis for a first of a new series of Bible Study books, and this volume will be ready later. But the other two series of Bible readings are both here, together with the very very best of the evening addresses. And once again, I had to remove a great deal of material, so if you want the parrot jokes, you will have to resort to the tapes. What is left is still absolutely excellent and I commend it to you.

Ali Hull
Bristol 2002

The Bible Readings

The Greatest Story Ever Told
John 17 – 21

by Bruce Milne

BRUCE MILNE

Bruce was born and raised in Dundee and was converted in his late teens during an evangelistic campaign. Sensing a call to full-time ministry, he studied Arts and Theology at St Andrews and London universities before serving as a church planter of a new congregation near Edinburgh. He taught at Spurgeons College before moving to Canada to become the Senior Minister of First Baptist Church, Vancouver, where he ministered for seventeen years. Bruce is currently engaged in writing, conference ministry and the encouragement of ministers. His best known book, *Know the Truth*, a basic introduction to theology, has been published in thirteen languages worldwide.

Intercession
Chapter 17:1 – 26

Introduction

I have entitled these chapters in John 'The Greatest Story Ever Told.' Remember how Paul writes that this is 'of first importance: that Christ died for our sins according to the Scriptures, that He was buried, that He was raised on the third day according to the Scriptures' (1 Cor. 15:3,4). There is nothing more important. I'm sure the Convention council were led in directing our attention this particular Keswick to the centre of our faith because this is the first Keswick since September 11th. The world has changed, subtly and yet truly. There is anxiety abroad that was not there before and we anticipate fearfully what horrors may lie ahead tomorrow. The danger of this kind of context is that we begin to allow these political realities, terrible and yet overwhelmingly important, to take centre stage, and the things that ultimately matter get moved towards the periphery. What ultimately matters is that here are things that are real, true and lasting beyond any political realities. As Dorothy L. Sayers put it, 'From the beginning of time until now into eternity, this is the only thing that has ever happened.'

Back in 1998 I was, for the very first time, in Jerusalem. I was doing a course at University College in Jerusalem for three weeks. I gazed across the panorama of the city. There was that hill, to my right, the Mount of Olives! Down there, that green patch … that's Gethsemane! There, the Via Dolorosa, and at the end of it, the Church of the Holy Sepulchre – Calvary! Nearby, the site of the tomb of Jesus! Suddenly, these almost indescribable feelings swept over me. My sins were there. Christ died for me there and rose again; my life was there. This is my second visit to Jerusalem! I was there two thousand years ago when Jesus died and rose again for me. The mystery of our incorporation into Christ, that is what every Christian can say. These are the things that determine us. We are Christ's, and Christ is our reality! His death and rising is what shapes and determines who we are in time and eternity.

The prayer of consecration

Chapter 17 – we begin at the deep end. Called, perhaps not wrongly, the 'Holy of Holies' of the New Testament, the setting, in verse 1, is 'After Jesus said this'. He's probably still in the upper room with the disciples. What is the 'this' – almost certainly the whole of that upper room discourse on the theme of the glorification of Son and Father (13:31). He's embracing all of that. After expounding the great truths to the disciples of the life of discipleship, He prays. John Calvin, I think, makes a helpful application of that when he says, 'Jesus here shows teachers an example that they should not only occupy them-selves in sowing the word, but, by mixing their prayers with it, should implore God's help that His blessing should make their work fruitful.' It's a moral for all teachers of the word; preaching plus prayer, instruc-tion plus intercession.

Would you like to revive the preaching ministry of your pastor? Here's how to do it. Next Sunday, back in your church, in that song before the sermon, slip away. Find a quiet room in the church, get down on your knees, pray and plead the blessing of God upon that ministry as your pastor is preaching. Better still, get two or three others who share that vision to go with you. Best of all, recruit about a dozen and then you can have a schedule through a month. If you start doing that, within a couple of weeks, your pastor will know the difference. Within a month, the congregation will know the difference. Within six weeks, the community will feel the difference.

Jesus prays for himself

Our Lord turns to prayer. The prayer divides very readily into three parts. Almost all the commentators agree with it:

- Jesus praying for Himself (verses 1-5)
- Jesus praying for the disciples (verses 6-19)
- Jesus praying for all Christians (verses 20-26)

First, for Himself. This indeed is holy ground. The person who reads the word spoken by one Person of the blessed Trinity to another Person must surely be prepared to find much that they cannot fully understand. Jesus begins, characteristically – 'Abba, abba!' It's unique to Jesus; in all the wealth of prayers and liturgies that have come down to us, there is nothing like this. Jesus stands absolutely alone as He comes into the Father's presence and He prays, and you know the meaning – 'Dadda!' It's a little child's word. There's nothing irreverent about that! This is honour, respect, trust, submission: all that Jesus teaches us we should have in prayers, caught so beautifully. And the wonder of it is that through the Holy Spirit we can pray, 'Abba, Father.'

'The time' – better 'the hour' – 'has come.' That's a signal word through this gospel: the hour is not yet (2:4), the hour is at hand (12:23). Now here the hour has come, the hour that is the central moment in the entire human story, in the life of the universe, in the self-revelation of God, in the plan of redemption, in our personal salvation. It's the hour of glorification of the Son and the Father through Him. Why does He ask for His own glorification? I think the sense of that is vindication. He knows what lies ahead. Remember that saying, 'I have a baptism to be baptised with' (Lk. 12:50). He knows what lies ahead; what terrible degradation, dishonour, dispersoning that He has to face; the utter self-immolation that lies before

Him. We will never know into eternity what this means. Facing that terror before Him, He reaches to the Father: 'Lift me out of it! Bring Me through! Glorify Your Son.' But it's not a self-preoccupation, it's in order that through this whole act of self-sacrifice, 'You may be glorified. Glorify Your name that the Son may glorify You.'

When people face death, their ultimate concerns necessarily surface. We were reminded of that so poignantly last September. Do you remember those terrible searing e-mail and telephone messages? 'Jim, the plane has been hijacked and it doesn't look good. I just want you to know I love you and I hope to see you again.' Or from New York, 'There's a fire on the floor, Jill. I love you so much.' In these moments, you don't talk about your ambitions, achievements and plans, they're trivia. You talk about what.matters; loyalties, the love of your life. As Jesus faces death, there emerges from His heart the ultimate motivation and longing. It's caught earlier in Gethsemane where Jesus says 'What shall I say? Father, save me from this hour?' (12:27). 'If it's possible, take this cup from Me … but for this purpose I've come to this hour.' It's like a vice – there's the front face, coming against Him, He's starting back – but then right behind Him, there is the thrust of the eternal destiny and purposes of God, thrusting Him forward, and the two faces of the vice close in and His whole person is broken up at the depths. Out of that depths there emerges that cry that expresses all His ultimate longings. 'Father,' He cries, 'Glorify Your name!' Heaven cannot keep silent and there's a reply, immediately: 'I have glorified it, and I will glorify it again.' When we can begin meaningfully to say, 'Father, glorify Your name' as a fundamental motivation of our life, we are beginning to mature as Christians, like Him.

Glorify Your name

The question is, how does He glorify the Father?. Two ways: first of all by the impartation of life (verses 2,3) and by the completion of work (verse 4). The glorification of the Son will be His exaltation to the place of supreme authority in the universe, within which and from which He is able to impart life. So the glorification of the Father through the Son is expressed in the imparting of life to sinners. Notice two features of this life; it is given, 'that He might give eternal life to all those you have given Him.' That's echoed a little later in the prayer (verses 6-9). Here is salvation from the perspective of heaven, as the Father and Son reflect upon it. It's salvation in terms of the purpose of God, that sovereign grace that has brought us salvation. The human responsibility is not denied and it appears elsewhere, but here, we see it from heaven's perspective. I don't think Christians have too great a difficulty with that. Salvation is His gift to us. Then the prayer goes on to talk about the substance of it: 'This is eternal life; that they may know You, the only true God, and Jesus Christ, Whom you have sent' (verse 3). Life knowing God; that's where you start the Christian life and that's where you finish it. Remember Paul in Philippians 3, 'All that I care for is to know Christ.' There is the heart of it all, knowing God, that brings glory to the Father.

Note here the link that is established between worship on the one hand, the glorifying of God, and evangelism on the other, the imparting of life. How can we glorify God? God is supremely glorified by the mission of the Son, sent into the world by the Father, which becomes the mission of the church, sent into the world by the Son. It's by the imparting of life that we glorify God. We must never, never separate evangelism and worship; evangelism *is* worship. If the heart of worship is seeking the honour of God, then how can we be indifferent to the fact that multitudes do not honour Him? If God's honour is bound up with our giving Him glory, then His dishonour is bound up with multitudes who withhold that glory. For the Lord's glory, for His honour, we are motivated to share the good news that people might enter into eternal life. Doesn't Paul say that? In 2 Corinthians 4 he says that as grace spreads to more and more people, so thanksgiving increases to the glory of God. We cannot have a passion for God that is biblically legitimate if we do not also have a passion for lost people. It means that our evangelism needs to be done worshipfully. We need to get away from all this self-promotion stuff and the numbers game. When you're evangelising, this is holy work, sharing the good news that others might bow and honour our blessed Lord. There is this holy alliance and we need to make sure we hold it together.

The second way in which God is with us is by the completion of work (verse 4): 'I have brought You glory on earth by completing the work You gave Me to do.' We notice the supreme motivation of that. When we get to heaven there will be a glory that we give to God, but only now do we have the possibility of glorifying Him on earth. Amid a broken, warring, rebel world, there is a special possibility in glorifying God. Notice there is limit. This is a great word to Christian leaders. If you're a Christian leader, you are not called upon to win the world for Christ. Don't misunderstand me. We will pray that the world comes to Christ. We do all we can to reach it. But the church is called to win the world to Christ and we are called to find out, within that total purpose of God, what our role is and do that with all our might. That glorifies God. Jesus is our model here because there were specific limitations set on Him. Geographically, He never reached the world, He was always confined within central Palestine. Think of the dimensions of life that He never entered into; He never knew the intimacies of marriage, the struggles of parenthood, the challenges of middle-age, the limitations of ageing. Even His teaching and healing ministry didn't touch multitudes in Palestine. It was probably the most thickly populated part of the world in the context of Jesus' life. Multitudes were either not healed or ministered to directly. Yet He brought glory to the Father because He did what He was called to do perfectly and completely with single-minded dedication and at the end He could say, 'I've glorified Your name.'

Jesus' prayer for Himself rounds off in verse 5 with this great statement: 'Father, glorify Me in Your presence with the glory I had with You before the world began.' It's not that our Lord is backing away from His incarnation, or all the depths of His identity with us and the passion. But He sees beyond that swirling flood to the Father's house and something of that emerges here in His humanity.

Jesus prays for His disciples

These men were important to Jesus. Our Lord called them His friends and I think we need to hear that. He prays for His friends. Note who they are; they're identified in terms of their ownership (verses 6,9), they belong to the Father, He's given them to the Son, and they have come out of the world, so they are partakers of a new life. They have been born again in terms of chapter 3, they have been regenerated, they have received a new kind of life.

Notice the claim that Jesus makes in the context of that, 'All I have is Yours,' He's talking about all those that have been given, 'All You have is Mine'(verse 10). That's a staggering claim. Don Carson, in his commentary, notes that this is a christological claim of extraordinary reach. They are those who have obeyed His word (verse 6). That's a strange thing, when you think of their very fragmented responses to Jesus. Carson argues they've obeyed in terms of the gospel they've received. It's unpacked in verse 8; 'For I gave them the words You gave me.' It's the confession that Jesus has come from God, that Jesus is Lord. Certainty in the Christian life, in the end, comes from resting on the words of Jesus, and notice it's the words, not just the ideas. It's verbal revelation. They have obeyed the word, they have received the revelation, and thirdly, astonishing, in verse 10, 'glory has come to Me through them.' We feel like tapping our Lord on the shoulder and saying, 'Do you mean that? This bunch?' They're about to flee and leave Him, they didn't understand his teaching, and they squabble about who was greatest. Peter denies Him, Judas betrays Him. Of course, Judas is no longer here, but does the quality of their response really deserve His comment, 'glory has come to Me through them'? I think J.C. Ryle is helpful: 'It's evident that Jesus sees far more in His believing people than they see in themselves or that others see in them.'

You know what that means? It means there is not a Christian whose view of themselves is higher than Jesus' view of them! He thinks so much of you. Can we not affirm what verse 23 says: that the love of the Father for us is equal to the love that He has for the Son? Can any not take to themselves those great words at Jesus' baptism, as the Father said, 'This is My son, this is my daughter, with whom I am well pleased?' If you feel that's too much, let's just say 'pleased'. Our heavenly Father looks down and He sees you, and says to all the host of heaven – 'That's My boy! That's My girl!' He loves us as He loves His Son. Even the weakest faith has value to Him. They are who He prays for.

Protection

What does He pray for them? Four things; first, that they may be protected (verse 11). They need to be protected because they have two formidable foes, firstly, the world, which has hated them (verse 14). Jesus had spelled that out in more detail in chapter 15:18-25. It's not that we go out of our way to make the world hate us; on the contrary, we love the world, we get involved in the world, we care for people, we're as winsome as we possibly can be in our witness; we don't go out to be hated… but inevitably, because we follow a different leader and our value system is different, necessarily, in loyalty to Him – we are hated. You can know that in the market place, the office, the classroom, the community; sometimes in the home. That's the cost, so we need protection from the world and its insidious assaults.

We also need protection from the evil one (verse 15). We must never underestimate our enemy; Jesus encountered a real opposition. There's mystery around the devil but the reality is so clear. I find in my Christian life, again and again, one of the greatest temptations is to forget the devil. We get all set up for the Lord in this great new programme, everything's in place and suddenly – what's all this? We need to say with the parable of Jesus, 'an enemy has done this'. Be alert to that and seek through prayer in the name of Christ to be protected.

'Protect them by the power of your name' (verse 11). The name of God is the revealed character of God, and so our protection is to commit ourselves to and to remind ourselves of who He is. 'The name of the Lord is like a strong tower', says Proverbs 18:10, 'and the righteous run to it and they're protected.' Protection is in the name of the Lord, in the character of God, in who God is, and that is what Jesus has been doing right through His ministry. He's revealing the Father. This prayer is a very good model of it, you can go through this prayer and see all the things about God that are taught us in this prayer; His Father's love, His sovereign purpose; that Jesus was sent by the Father; His ownership of His people, the indwelling Christ … It's in these things, as we lay hold of them and affirm them, that we find our protection.

Secondly, it's corporate protection. Notice the linkage in verse 11: 'so that they may be one as We are one'. It's not just vertical, with the Lord, but it's horizontal within His people. Sometimes I think we represent the Christian life, the life of victory, the life in the Spirit, the overcoming life, in too individualistic terms. We've forgotten sometimes that all the basic New Testament teaching about living the victorious Christian life is given in letters to churches. This whole thing is to be understood corporately. The Christian life is envisaged not in isolated individual terms but in terms of a commitment to a community where we are loved, prayed for, supported and encouraged. It's in the community that there is the strength and the protection as well.

Delight

Thirdly, that they be delighted (verse 13). There is a beautiful balance here. Amid all the grim, costly conflict of the Christian disciple's life, you get this: 'I am coming to You ... but I say these things while I'm still in the world, so that they might have the full measure of My joy in them'. Our Lord wants His disciples to have joy! Jesus wants us to have joy, deep within, that joy of the kingdom, the joy of Christ, the joy of His resurrection, His presence, heaven and the victories of His grace; the joy that He had as He went to the cross. It's not running away from life, it's facing life.

Mission

Finally, He prays that they may be dedicated to the mission in the world. Being set apart for the mission is enabled on two fronts. Through the truth (verse 17); disciples can only be set apart for the service of God by living in and under the truth of God illumined by the Spirit of God. The other enablement is verse 19: 'For them I sanctify Myself'. Jesus lays Himself upon the altar. It's in His sanctification that we find the resources for our being set apart for the sake of the world. That's a very holy moment; here is the Son, coming again to the Father, in self-giving. It's terribly important to see that though our Lord came out of eternity and the purpose of God to give Himself, and although He reaffirmed that again and again through His mission, yet here He comes to the cross and once again there is a need for yet another moment of commitment. We sometimes talk about giving our lives to God but you can't give your life to God in one moment. All you can give is that moment. It takes a lifetime to give a lifetime to God. That's why the Lord's Supper is given to us, a place of recommitment and renewal.

Jesus prays for all Christians

That's us, isn't it? We've all believed through their message. We're part of His prayer. He prays that we be united (verses 21-23) – that they 'may be one, Father, just as You are in Me and I am in You.' Again in verse 22, 'that they [may] be one as We are' and 'I in them and You in Me. May they be brought to complete unity' (verse 23). Three things about that unity: it is supernatural; given by the Spirit – we are born again and therefore share this common life of God; it is tangible because the world has to believe through it and so it has to be seen; and it is evangelical. It is believing on the basis of the revelation that Jesus has given. Don Carson's commentary appropriately observes it is not simply a unity of love; it is a unity predicated on adherence to the revelation of the Father through His Son. There are moments, despite our commitment to and our longing for this unity, where we may necessarily have to say 'no' if we feel the revelation of God through Jesus is in question.

We do everything we can to maintain this unity so that the world may believe. The world believing is so critical. The place where this teaching is most immediately relevant is where the world encounters the church; and that is in the local church. It's there as they're brought into a service and they contact the prayer group or an Alpha group or whatever. It's there we need to have this unity that is persuasive of the reality of Christ and His love.

We're living in a time when God has stirred up His world. Everywhere today, especially in the cities but it's all through societies and cultures, there is huge diversity. That is creating massive problems, socially. How do you live with your neighbour when your neighbour is different from you and in the light of September 11th, where your neighbour may be your enemy? What a marvellous opportunity it gives to the church today evangelistically, if we can only embody the values of the kingdom and live out communities of love and accept-ance across all these differences, and not simply reflect all the divisions of the world. What a relevant witness we can have, that's what Jesus is saying. 'By this shall all men know that you are My disciples,' says Jesus, 'if you have love', and that's agape love, that accepts difference. He prays finally that His mission may be completed (verses 24-26), by our sharing and seeing His glory. There's the prayer of Jesus.

Calvin, at the very beginning, gave us one application of why this prayer is here. It's to help us realise that teaching must also have prayer mixed with it. But I want to press that question in a more profound way. Why does the Holy Spirit give us this prayer at this point in the biblical record? Let me refer you back to chapter 16 of this gospel, and verse 23, 'I tell you the truth, My Father will give you whatever you ask in My name. ... Ask and you will receive, that your joy may be complete.' Jesus is saying that prayer in Jesus' name is guaranteed an answer. The answer may be 'no' , but God will always answer prayer in Jesus' name. If God commits himself to answer our prayer in Jesus' name, how much more will He answer Jesus' prayer in Jesus' name? That's what this is all about. It is Jesus on the brink of His self-sacrifice, throwing His arms around all the generations of the people of God, all our witness, our mission, our ministry, our service and our faith, He gathers it all up in His mighty arms and presents it before the Father. Therefore all of that is secured. God the Father says 'Amen' to it; the prayer of Jesus is irresistible. Despite calamities, bombs, ter-ror, trauma and martyrdom, we will be protected, united, delighted, dedicated, completed, glorified, because Jesus has prayed for us. If that does not encourage you then nothing I say could do it.

In the book of Revelation which John was inspired to write, years later, in the seventh chapter, we're given a wonderful picture of the people of God. There they are, from every people, nation, language and tongue, celebrating, praising, dressed in white robes. Have you ever thought about this: that John saw you? If you're a Christian, you have already been seen in glory and you're wonderfully happy, totally purified and very beautiful. The Lord Jesus Christ is your life, glory, joy and praise. Hallelujah!

Confrontation
Chapter 18:1 – 40

Introduction

As we come into chapter 18, we should note the change as far as the material we are dealing with is concerned. Yesterday we were dealing with closely argued teaching, albeit in the form of prayer, but now we move to gripping narrative, punctuated by dialogue and occasional comment by the evangelist. That form of material will be with us to the end of the series. As we come into chapter 18 you get a sense of foreboding in that dark night in Jerusalem. It's like that stifling feeling just before an electric storm breaks, and there's a certain sense of inevitability about all this. Jesus has come from the Father into the world, He must leave the world to return to the Father, at great and terrible cost. Only so can the darkness be confronted, His own be liberated and the Father glorified.

The arrest of Jesus (verses 1-11)

If the traditional sites in Jerusalem are correct, then Jesus with the disciples faced the journey of about a mile, moving northward and then turning eastward past the great dark outline of the temple. Emerging through the Lion's gate they would snake their way down the path, across the shallow valley of the Kidron. Not far up would bring them to the garden area of Jerusalem, where the rich had their places of rest. Obviously some rich benefactor made his garden available to Jesus regularly. Critically, it was a place where Judas could find them.

Having sprung the trap, sent Judas on his foul errand, Jesus now awaits, offering Himself for capture. He kneels there in what we know as the Garden of Gethsemane, awaiting His arrest. What overwhelmed me as I saw the topography for the first time is this simple and yet profoundly touching truth: Jesus knelt on the road to escape. The road of the Mount of Olives runs on to Bethany at the top. Just a quick command to the disciples, a scramble, another twenty minutes up that slope and they would be with friends. A few quickly saddled horses and they could be off, northward, through the night, to Galilee and to safety. On the very road to escape, He knelt – for us – and awaited His arrest.

He prays on through the night. John doesn't give us anything of the detail of the Gethsemane praying; but there's a hint of it in verse 11: 'Shall I not drink the cup the Father has given Me?' At last, He sees what He anticipates (verse 3); torches and lanterns emerging from the city. It's an interesting group; three elements in it, all eerily familiar to us today. There are the soldiers; an attachment would mean some thousand foot soldiers if it was all of the attachment, certainly several hundred. This was the Roman force, normally garrisoned at the coast at Caesarea, who came up to Jerusalem for the feast times, because of the great potential for disturbance then. Here was a considerable force, fully armed. Jesus' powers were known and there was much sympathy among the people who would know the implications of arresting Him. We have here the representatives of oppressive political and military rule and with them the officials from the chief priests and Pharisees. Here are the representatives of corrupt religion; and that too is familiar. If you share your faith today you will know that for many people 'religion' has become a bad word. September 11th has contributed no doubt to that, but that's where we are. Let's be clear, corrupt religion in most people's minds does not exclude Christianity and our record is far from pure.

Thirdly is Judas, representing personal betrayal. This dark and terrible triumvirate of evil come together – the encounter is at hand. And apparently darkness wins. Verse 12 has Jesus bound and being taken away under arrest, strangely vulnerable, submissive to the powers of darkness.

That is only on the surface, as John would have us know, and we're given hints of some other dimensions. For example, there is Jesus' initiative mentioned in verse 4. Jesus went out to them. Our Lord is still in control, knowing all that was going to happen to Him. What is the source of that knowledge? Is it the illumination of the Spirit in His mind and heart? That's possible. But I think it's very striking when you study the passion narratives how prominent is the sense of fulfilment of Scripture. Again and again you get it: 'that the Scriptures might be fulfilled.' Amidst all the miracles of this great climax to Jesus' life and ministry, the writers of the Scripture never lose sight of another miracle: the miracle of the word of God being fulfilled in the midst of it all. He knew from the Scriptures all that was going to happen to Him.

Then there's Jesus' identity: He goes out to them. 'Who is it you want?' 'Jesus of Nazareth.' 'I am He,' He says. Just two words in the Greek – it's a great self-definition, a sense of God; it links right through this gospel, with the 'I am' sayings. Exodus: 'I am that I am', and Isaiah 40 to 55, 'I am the Lord, there is no other; I am God alone' and so on. The effect is dramatic (verse 6); they drew back, and fell to the ground. Something of the deity of our Lord breaks through. Remember what happened at Nazareth, how they took Him to the top of that hill to cast Him down and the Scripture says, 'He passed through their midst' (Lk. 4:30). His hour was not yet, and so He moves through them, the authority of His deity there.

The other side of the triumph of darkness

Here is Jesus' purpose. Firstly, verse 8: 'If you are looking for me ... let these men go.' Here are the terms for Jesus' arrest, He will give Himself up to them provided they guarantee safety and the freedom of His followers. This happened in fulfilment of the Scripture, 'I've not lost one of them,' but there's a profound insight here. Here is the whole atoning act of God in Jesus Christ. As Jesus allows Himself to be imprisoned so that His followers may be set free, He draws upon Himself all the malignancies of evil that they may pass from us by His grace.

Secondly, His purpose in verse 11; there's a bit of a skirmish in the garden there, a servant loses an ear. Jesus, we know from the other gospels, heals, and then speaks to Peter – 'Put your sword away. Can I not ask the Father and He will immediately give us twelve legions of angels?' 'Shall I not drink the cup the Father has given Me?'

What is this cup? For anyone who knows their Old Testament, the cup has only one possible meaning. It's the cup of God's wrath. For example Isaiah 51: 'Jerusalem, you … have drunk from the … cup of His wrath'. Or Jeremiah 25: 'Take from My hand this cup filled with the wine of My wrath'; Zechariah 12 as well. What is the cup? What does He fear, what does He struggle with? Is it death? No. Is it Satan? No. He's cast out. Is it the Holy One becoming sin? That certainly is an unspeakable possibility. He made Him to be sin for us. But surely this is the heart of it. The cup is the Father in His wrath. We have to be very careful how we state this in terms of the Trinity and not lose that sense of unity of the Godhead, but in some mysterious profound way, it is the Father whom Jesus starts back from, for He must bear the wrath of heaven. Remember that flaming sword back in Genesis chapter 3, set to guard the road to the tree of life, so that the very presence of God, for us in our sin, becomes a threat to us. That flaming sword, God must take in His grace and thrust it into His own heart, and extinguish it there for us. An amazing, amazing love. That's what He fears. Is that why He prays at the cross, 'My God, My God, why have You forsaken Me?' No 'Abba'. The only prayer of Jesus without the Abba. This is deep. The gospel may be free but it's not cheap, it may be simple, but it's not superficial. He faces that, and as He goes to His arrest and all that follows it, He is going to take that cup of wrath from the Father's hand so that He might drink it to the dregs for us.

The Jewish trial and Peter's denials

From this point the chapter has five sections:
- Annas part 1 (verses 12-14)
- Peter's first denial (verses 15-18)
- Annas part 2 (verses 19-24)
- Peter's denials 2 and 3 (verses 25-27)
- The Gentile world, Pilate and the first part of the Roman trial (verses 28-40)

Annas part 1 (verses 12-14)

They took Him first to Annas, the father-in-law of Caiaphas the high priest. Annas' position is very significant. He actually was the high priest through Jesus' adolescence. At that time He went up to the temple (Lk. 2) for the first time; probably Annas was the one who had presided at that celebration and now here he is. Now why? Surely Jesus should go to Caiaphas? But Annas cannot let the power go, and he remains the power behind the throne, as one after another of his sons and finally his son-in-law are high priest.

Annas represents the rather pathetic picture of an old man hanging on to power. It's not easy in Christian ministry to relinquish power, yet it has to be done. God gives grace for it. We finish His work, and that glorifies Him, but there is a finishing point, a relinquishing and a passing on. The tragedy of hanging on to power beyond the appropriate moment is well illustrated by Annas. By hanging on to power, he becomes personally implicated in the darkest moment in the whole history of Israel; the rejection and crucifixion of the Messiah.

Peter's first denial (verses 15-18)

Before we get any further with that we switch back to Peter and the other disciple (verse 15) who, arguably, was John the evangelist. He has an 'in' with the high priest and so he gets in; by his good offices Peter is allowed, also, to enter. Peter, at this point, totally discomfited and totally thrown, can't understand what's happening. It's dark and in the high priest's courtyard he's out of his familiar territory. He's not in any sense in a comfortable environment and there's this lassie on the door.

She speaks to him. 'You're not one of His disciples, are you?' 'I am not'
he says. Fatally, he crosses the line. He denies Jesus. Watch and pray.
Peter's unguarded; he denies His Lord. It's cold and there's a fire there
and Peter now complicates his situation by fraternising with the
enemy and stands round the fire to keep warm.

Annas part 2 (verses 19-24)

Then we're back with the high priest and the interrogation by Annas.
This is a preliminary hearing. Annas is trying to get a basis for the
charge that they'll bring to the Sanhedrin when it meets a little later;
it's still early morning. So Jesus is questioned about His teaching and
His disciples. Back in Deuteronomy we get the reason for this line of
questioning: 'If a prophet, or one who foretells by dreams, appears
among you and announces to you a miraculous sign or wonder, and
if the sign or wonder of which he has spoken takes place, and he says,
"Let us follow other gods" … "and let us worship them" … That
prophet or dreamer must be put to death, because he preached rebellion against the LORD your God' (Deut. 13:1,2,5).

Here's the prophet, Jesus, He's come and the signs unfortunately are
real, these miracles have happened, but isn't He saying, 'Come and follow another God? Isn't He taking people away from the worship of
the true God?' That's what Annas is seeking to prove. But Jesus won't
answer in detail about His teaching, He simply reminds Annas that all
that He said has been there and available. 'Why question Me?' (verse
21) 'Ask those who heard Me.'

Jewish jurisprudence was built upon the testimony of witnesses and
so the witnesses should have been in the garden to accuse Jesus
and certainly witnesses should have been the ones interrogated by
Jewish law to establish their credibility and then their testimony
would be taken in. Jesus is asking for a fair trial. He's exposing the
falsehood of all of this, the conniving, the suppression of law and due
process. At that, one of the officials who doesn't like the way Jesus
addresses the great Annas, leans forward and slaps Him across the face.
Jesus' reply, notice, 'If I said something wrong, testify what's wrong.
But if I spoke the truth, why do you strike me?' I think it's worth
noting that incarnate grace can still expose evil.

Annas can get nowhere. The implacable integrity of Jesus is impregnable and so he sends Him on to Caiaphas the high priest. That will in turn lead to a meeting of the Sanhedrin which John doesn't report; he's complementing the other gospels. There's a signal of that in verse 14, with reference to Caiaphas as the one who had advised the Jews it was good if one man die for the people, that's a signal back to chapter 11, the report there of an earlier meeting of the Sanhedrin which concluded with the decision to seek the death of Jesus. John doesn't need to repeat that and the other gospels have it, but you remember the detail: as our Lord is arraigned, witnesses are brought and they can't agree. Finally Jesus is put under oath to reply when He refuses to make an answer: 'Are you the Christ, the Son of the blessed?' 'I am! And you will see the Son of Man coming in the clouds of heaven' – that great figure from Daniel, the instrument of God's eternal judgements and destiny. 'You have heard the blasphemy!' they all cry and condemn Him as worthy of death for the blasphemy of claiming to be the Son of God.

Peter's denials 2 and 3 (verses 25-27)

Peter's warming himself and someone else turns. 'You're not one of His disciples, are you?' He said it once, it's easier to say the second time. 'I am not.' Then finally, a little more threatening now; a relative of the man he wounded in the garden: 'Didn't I see you with Him in the olive grove?' 'No, not me. I don't know this man' – with oaths and curses. The cock crew. Suddenly Peter remembered and Luke tells us that he went out and wept bitterly.

There is a great lesson taught us in this section (verses 15-31). Notice how we move back and forward between the interrogation of Annas and Peter's denials. What we have here is a hugely important point: over against the faithfulness of Jesus is the unfaithfulness of Peter. In the light of Jesus' faithfulness, Peter's unfaithfulness stands exposed. Raymond Brown, the Catholic commentator says, 'John has constructed a dramatic contrast wherein Jesus stands up to His questioners and denies nothing, while Peter cowers before his questioners and denies everything.' It's in the light of Jesus' action as He takes our place and stands for us in His blessed integrity and faithfulness that our unfaithfulness and denials stand. It's a very important principle, a question that is very relevant to our own time, of the way we know sin. How do we come to a conviction that we are sinners? Ultimately the Holy Spirit brings that conviction but how does the Spirit work in that? That's very relevant to our time because a conviction of sin is not particularly widespread, nor is it particularly focused. If I can quote just a sentence or two from Charles Price and Ian Randall's *Transforming Keswick*

> Modern concepts of right and wrong are no longer seen in the black and white terms they once were. There is much more that is perceived as grey and much more tolerance in our thinking. We are less shockable. Guilt is not generally regarded as a healthy emotion. Our consciences are consequently less sensitised. Addressing the conscience is not as common a feature of preaching as it once was and maybe not even as acceptable.

Every preacher faces this challenge. How do we facilitate, be available to the Spirit, in awakening conscience and the sense of sin? I suspect that very widely we identify sin with a feeling of sin – you become a sinner by feelings. But the trouble is, as all of us know who are involved with pastoral ministry, feelings vary enormously and immediately you get into the whole business of diverse personalities. There are certain people who always feel guilty. You make an appeal in the church and you can tell who's going to come forward! Almost. That's not to eliminate God's working. I inherited a situation in my church where appeals were made every week. I went with that for a little while, but I began to find I could tell who was coming, week after week. it wasn't particularly helpful to them or to anyone else. Thankfully the Lord went on saving people so we didn't need this.

Sinners by faith

For many years I struggled with this and then one day light came to me as I was reading in Martin Luther, where he talks about becoming a sinner by faith; not by feelings but by faith. He's talking about the principle that's illustrated in this chapter: it's in the light of grace, the light of God dealing with our sin, that we see sin exposed. I look away objectively to Christ and that is where we see our sin. How we feel about it is almost irrelevant. There I am taught who I am because of what was done for me on the cross. This is hugely important because we come to the cross, and see Jesus dying there, spread-eagled on the cross writhing in agony and finally, as my sin is laid upon Him, crying out in the darkness, 'My God, my God, why have You forsaken Me?' – there I see what I need. I need that every moment. There's who I am, I am one who needs the blessed substitutionary work of Jesus every moment for my standing before God.

Nothing we do is perfect. That's why Jesus in His whole self is given for us because our whole self needs to be atoned for. I find myself confessing with Paul that in my flesh dwells no good thing. That's Romans 7 and Paul can say that because in Romans 5 and earlier he has expounded the cross: God demonstrating His love for us, in that while we were sinners, Christ died for us. You come to an understanding of sin by faith. As we see Christ die for us, we say: 'I am that person who every moment needs that atoning sacrifice, that Person of the Son of God in my place for me.' I am a sinner. I don't need to feel it. It's a fact in the light of God's salvation and His grace. This truth establishes our identity and identity is so important in Christian living and maturity.

If you say 'That's a terribly pessimistic view of human nature', the other side is also there – that same cross that slays me is the cross that revives me. It puts me down, it lifts me up, because the cross tells me how valuable I am to God, how much God loves me. If I and you were on sale in God's universe, on the price tag He would put the cross. On the one hand we're utterly slain, on the other hand we're marvellously affirmed. We learn who we are at the cross. Every moment we live by grace, we live by Christ, we are before God in Him. Utterly sinners, utterly lost, utterly damned, and yet marvellously saved, affirmed, held and sanctified.

Post-modern society
Not just for identity, this is hugely important for ministry. We go to a society that is several generations into post-Christianity and its value systems are a long way from the value systems of the gospel. There are

pockets that are exceptional but that's where we're at. It's certainly where we are in Canada. It's total secularisation and the result is, if we're going to reach this world for Christ, we have got to learn to handle people who come to us with a lifestyle that is very different to the one taught in the Scriptures. We have to learn to relate to people in a way that, while it calls them to repentance, does not set us apart from them as superior because they've got a marvellous nose for that. Paul Tournier, a Christian therapist, says this

> How many times I have thought about it when a man has been sobbing in my consulting room as he has given expression to his disappointment with himself, his faults and failures, his despair, his feelings of inferiority, that he is nearer to the kingdom of God than I who listen to him. And I come nearer to the kingdom as well as to the man only insofar as I recognise that I am as guilty, as powerless, as inferior, and as desperate as he is. Only then can I help him for I am delivered from all spirit of judgement, I am his companion in repentance and in waiting for grace.

If you're involved in sharing the faith and in counselling, you'll know immediately how authentic that is. But how do we come to people in such a way that we don't pass judgement, and cause them to run away because of our superior self-righteous spirit? This is how we get there, by seeing ourselves in the light of the cross.

Just for a moment, let me speak as a fool. We had a man who came to our congregation in Vancouver some years ago. He came late one night and we soon got on to the real thing. It all came pouring out ... a very sad and sordid story. All the time he was sharing all this he was looking into my eyes. At the end of it, it was my privilege to tell him that as he repented, there was grace in God, he could be forgiven; Christ had died for his sin. That was a little bit much for him to take in that night but he kept coming and some months later we had the great joy of baptising him; he joined our church, and then he moved away to another part of Canada. A few months later a letter arrived.

He shared the news that things were going wonderfully well, his marriage was back on course, he had a great new job, he was at a local

church and since then that he's held the road. But then he said this –
I paraphrase

> That night I came to your study and told you my story about my past
> and about what I'd done, I was looking very carefully at you and if you
> had shown the slightest quiver of contempt, rejection or dismissal of
> me because of what I'd done, do you know what I was going to do? I
> was going to stop the interview, I was going to leave your study,
> I was going to walk through Vancouver to the Lion's Gate bridge
> and I was going to throw myself off.

Isn't it good sometimes you don't know what you're dealing with in
ministry? I don't set myself up – that's why I say I talk as a fool – I
struggle with this as much as anybody. He represents this generation
and we have got to learn to love people, to help them to repentance
and new life, and that can only be done if we recognise that we are as
guilty, as powerless and as desperate as they are. You only learn that at
the cross. Living at the cross, being identified by the death of
Jesus, means that we are freed to reach this broken needy world in
Jesus' name. In the light of grace we see sin.

The Gentile world, Pilate and the first part of the Roman trial (verses 28-40)

In verse 28, you've got the verdict at the Jewish level, and it's a verdict
of blasphemy. Jesus must die. But there are two tiers of authority in
Palestine in the first century, and that verdict needs to be confirmed
by Pilate, the Roman governor. They don't want to go to see the
governor in his house; it's a pagan house and they would become ceremonially unclean. The Passover is already underway and they don't
want to be spoiled for celebrating the rest of the Passover. To be clean,
as they plot the death of the Son of the God, they will not enter the
Gentile house.

Pilate meets them outside. 'What charges are you bringing?' I think
it's almost certain there's been a connection with Pilate in the night,
perhaps with his officials if Pilate was still asleep and they understood

that Pilate would simply confirm their decision and deliver Jesus immediately up for crucifixion. But Pilate will not be twisted, he will not bow to their will, and he will conduct his own inquiry, thank you. So when he says 'Take Him and judge Him by your own law', Pilate's pushing their noses into the dirt, reminding them they don't have that right. Rome is master! But all this happens that the words spoken (verse 32) might be fulfilled. Christ will die on a cross. That's their purpose too, because the law had said, 'Cursed is everyone that hangs on a tree.' A Messiah who died on a cross at the hands of the Gentiles was about as possible as a square circle! That would end all this 'Jesus stuff' right there. That was their goal.

They pressed for crucifixion, but Pilate will conduct his examination. By 'Are you the King of the Jews?' he's asking, 'How do you plead, guilty or not guilty?' 'Is that your own idea?' Jesus is reaching for the man behind the proconsul. 'What do you think about me, Pilate? Am I a Jew?'

Then He talks about His kingdom. 'My kingdom is not of this world,' says Jesus. 'Rome need not fear from Me at the political level, the military level, that's not how My kingdom is established. My kingdom is from another place.' ... 'So You are a king.' 'Yes, I am. A king of truth.' And that helps us not to misinterpret verse 36 as though it means that we should have nothing to do with the political sphere in this political world. It's a kingdom of truth and truth is universal. Every area of life is infected by the issue of truth and we should be concerned for truth everywhere. The essence of the kingdom is not established by political power or maintained by military force.

'What is truth?' Cynical perhaps, but maybe just something there of a longing, and Pilate's done his examination. He's reached his conclusion and says, 'I find no basis for a charge against Him.' That should have ended the trial. It would have left Pilate unpopular but just. But he thinks of a card he can play and so he suggests, 'Maybe I should release Jesus as my amnesty prisoner.' That would show that Jesus was guilty, so would please these leaders and it would show him as a man of clemency, for the people, he was pretty sure, didn't share their view of Jesus. That's his offer, and he's surprised by the result. 'No, not Him. Give us Barabbas!' The text goes on in the other gospels – 'What then will I do with Jesus Who is called the Christ?' 'Crucify Him!'

The trial of humanity

Notice that a large part of this chapter and the way in which John presents Jesus and his approach to His death is in a legal key. He is arraigned as our Lord, accused of blasphemy by the Jews, accused of treason, rivalling Caesar, by the Roman authority. The trial of Jesus is the trial of humanity. Because we are the guilty. God's law has been spoken to us in conscience, in Scripture, in Christ, creation – and we've broken that law. All of us. What that law-breaking consists of is revealed to us in Genesis, the very first sin: two things. It consisted of blasphemy – 'you shall be as gods' – our aspiring to be our own God – and treason. 'You shall not eat of the tree' and they ate, breaking the law of God, rebelling against His proper and real authority. Blasphemy and treason are actually at the heart of all our sinning. The very charges that Jesus faced are the charges that we face and suddenly we see the whole trial of Jesus in a new light. Pilate, Caiaphas and Annas fall into the background and Jesus stands at the judgement seat of God, on our behalf. The charges we face, He faces for us. Isn't that part of the reason why He is silent at His trial and will not defend Himself? He is standing there for us. The judgement that is passed on Him becomes the judgement that ought to be passed on us. At Calvary He becomes the condemned for us. The blasphemy and treason which is our guilt is borne by Him and He dies for us.

That application is caught perfectly in the man whose name appears in the last verse of the chapter – Barabbas. Barabbas was justly tried and found guilty. It's only imagination that has Barabbas stagger out into that barrack courtyard and see Jesus and the cross thrust cruelly upon His bleeding back. Perhaps Barabbas finds himself that afternoon in the region of Calvary, and looking up at that central cross, he says, 'I should be there. He's dying for me.'

Oblation
Chapter 19:1 – 42

We come this morning to the climax of the greatest story ever told. The chapter falls into five sections:

- The second part of the Roman trial (verses 1-16)
- The crucifixion itself (verses 17-27)
- The death of Jesus (verses 28-30)
- The piercing of His side (verses 31-37)
- The burial of Jesus (verses 38-42)

The second part of the Roman trial (verses 1-16)

Pilate had offered the crowd the alternative of Jesus or Barabbas, and they had chosen Barabbas. Pilate, desiring to free Jesus who He knows is being unjustly condemned, decides on another resort to try to please the crowd. He has Jesus flogged. The Roman floggings were proverbial for their barbarity. The most terrible of all was routinely administered as part of the preliminary to crucifixion. The victim was stripped, bound to a pillar, and beaten by a number of torturers until the latter grew tired and the flesh of the victim hung in bleeding shreds. In the provinces such as Judea this was the task of soldiers. In the case of slaves or criminals such as Jesus, scourges or whips were used, the leather thongs often fitted with a spike or several pieces of bone or lead joined to form a chain. It's not surprising to hear that prisoners frequently collapsed and died under this procedure.

But there immediately follows another refinement of cruelty. Jesus, having been flogged by these Romans, is now their plaything. The hatred of the Romans for the Jews was well known. They had no time for the Jews. All the pent-up frustrations and hatred of the Roman soldiers now had an opportunity to be unleashed. 'We've got a king here ... a king needs a crown.' Not that imitation laurel wreath so often seen in Christian pictures but the spikes of the date palm, eight to ten inches long, twisted together and thrust cruelly into Jesus' head. 'A king must have a robe!' A robe is found and thrown round His shoulders and a sceptre too, the other evangelists mention this. It doesn't take much imagination to think what happens in a male barracks, does it? They come forward, one by one, bowing before Jesus in imitation homage to Caesar. They spit, punch and kick. When they're done, they hand Him back and Pilate presents Him to the Jews, hoping that this pathetic bleeding figure, as He staggers out from the hands of the soldiers, will somehow evoke their pity. Perhaps this is enough to satisfy them. But if that's Pilate's hope, it is quickly shown to be unfounded.

Jesus before Pilate

It has to be noted that the two trials are different as far as the charges were concerned. The first, before the Sanhedrin, was the blasphemy charge; He claimed to be the Son of God. But that wouldn't have worn well with the Romans for whom that would have just been a local superstition, so they change tack and present Jesus as a threat to Caesar and so the charge is treason. But at this point they revert to their blasphemy charge and it really gets to Pilate. He's immediately afraid. Cynical but also, like many Romans, he's profoundly superstitious. Maybe it was that message from his wife about her nightmares concerning this man – for whatever reason, he decides to interrogate Jesus further. Is this a divine man? So he asks Jesus about His origins: 'Where are you from?' He's been impressed by Jesus. This is more than man before him. But Jesus refuses to answer. Pilate is astonished. 'Don't you realise, I've power to release You?' 'No,' says Jesus, 'You actually have no power. Neither you nor your Caesar nor all your Roman armies, you couldn't lay a finger on Me unless it were given you from above. But as far as human responsibility is concerned, those who handed Me over to you bear greater guilt.' The Jews, those who had had the light of special revelation, all the Scriptures – responsibility is related to opportunity. Theirs is a greater sin.

Pilate now is determined to try and get Jesus off, and then the Jews, longing to get the thing to a head, produce their trump card. They shout out, 'If you let this man go, you are no friend of Caesar!' 'Friend of Caesar' was actually an honorific title in the empire, granted to certain people. Pilate had been given it, 'friend of Tiberias', because of the good offices of a very highly placed official in Rome, Sejanus – who had now fallen out of favour and been executed. Pilate's position was at this point probably very threatened. To get back to Rome with the news that he'd failed to deal firmly with a threat to Caesar's rule among the Jews … it might be the end of his life. Suddenly the trial of Jesus takes on a wholly new dimension for Pilate. It's not now Barabbas or Jesus. It's Jesus or Pilate! His whole life's at stake. That resolves it: from this moment, Jesus is as good as dead.

Pilate immediately brings out the judgement seat, struggling to have some remaining shred of credibility. He tries to mock them for a last time: 'This is your King,' he says, displaying Jesus. 'Crucify Him!' 'Crucify your King?' 'We have no King but Caesar.' And that is a faithful utterance on the part of those official representatives of the Jewish theocracy. It represents nothing less than the rending of the sacred covenant with God. Nothing was more fundamental to Jewish religion than the conviction that God and God alone was King; their King and the King of the world. No invading armies or plundering civilisation was ever able to eradicate that conviction from their hearts, and secure in that conviction that God was their King, they waited patiently for the coming of the Messiah who would bring in the kingdom in its fullness. Now, in this terrible moment of apostasy, these trusted leaders of God's people violate the sacred trust. Centuries of anticipation are thrown aside: 'We have no King but Caesar!' George Beasley Murray appropriately comments: 'It is nothing less than the abandonment of the Messianic hope of Israel.'

Pilate would have pronounced the words of sentence. But before we follow down that Via Dolorosa with Jesus let me pause around the words in verse 5: 'Here is the man!' One of the concerns of John in writing his gospel was to combat the incipient Gnosticism that was creeping into the culture and which would eventually become a major challenge for Christian theology. At its heart was a framework that separated matter and spirit. Matter was the source of all evil, and therefore incarnation in principle was impossible. Not so, says John. In the beginning was the Word, the Word was with God, the Word was God, and the Word became flesh. It's here as He goes to His death that His incarnation comes into fullest focus. These issues don't occupy us today, but this truth still resonates. We live in a suffering world. Scott Peck caught it brilliantly at the beginning of his book, *The Road Less Travelled*, one of the best first sentences in all literature, 'Life is difficult.' Research done recently in North America found that your average preacher needs to know that of the people in front of them, 80 per cent are living in quiet desperation. Life's difficult. Apart from the struggles of life, there are also these great devastating sorrows that sweep from time to time into everybody's experience. Beyond that, the agony of pain, the darkness of the world in our time, and we feel and live with it day by day. In a world like that, where do we turn?

Some people turn to religion. Some people turn to nature. Here's a quote from Ruskin, at the time of his personal tragedy: 'Oh that someone had told me in my youth, when all my heart seemed to be set on those colours and clouds, how little love of them would serve me when the silence of lawn and wood and the dews of morning should be completed and all my thoughts should be of those who by neither I was to meet more.' If only someone had told him in his youth nature can't do it … what about art? Heine, that great German poet, goes into the Louvre in Paris hoping to find, amid the great art treasures of the world, solace for his breaking heart. He's found apparently kneeling in front of the exquisite statue of the Venus de Milo and amid his sobs he blurts out, 'It's beautiful, but it has no arms!' But the cross has arms. Two arms outstretched to save. We have a God who has come down His mountain into the valley. In our hours of dereliction, He is there.

Jesus and suffering

What about His identity with our sufferings in this passage? Notice three aspects of it. First there was physical suffering; it's interesting we have a word in English – 'excruciating'. Do you know what that word literally means? *Ex-crucis.* It means 'pain of the cross'; a new word for a new depth of pain. He understands. Then there's relational suffering; the soldiers, their beating, their abusing, their hatred, their mockery, and the crowds chanting, 'Crucify, crucify!' and the Jewish leaders at the cross pouring contempt on Him. Maybe you're in a marriage with destructive patterns in it. At the physical level, we draw a veil over what happened to Jesus in that barracks, but it certainly was not nice. Physical abuse, we're aware of it today; out in western Canada where I am, recently there has been shock in the community: three high school kids, one after another, different schools, different contexts, have taken their own lives because of bullying. We estimate now apparently that more than half of kids in school are bullied. I don't know what the figures are for the UK but they're probably comparable.

When we come on to sexual abuse, our figures for North America are one girl in four, one boy in five. Perhaps the most depressing statistic is that for Christian homes and schools and communities, actually the statistics are exactly the same. This would be an astonishing gathering if there were not many of you who know exactly what I'm talking about – that evil self-centred desecration of your personal identity and intimacy. You've had counselling but it still lingers, your whole life is almost blighted by it. Listen, He knows, He understands, He's been there.

The crucifixion itself (verses 17–27)

Jesus carries His own cross, almost certainly only the cross-piece. Normally the upright was already in place in cities within the empire; crucifixions were depressingly commonplace. He staggers along that road, with help from Simon of Cyrene as the gospels indicate, as – no doubt overwhelmed with shock for His loss of blood and other effects of His injuries – He collapses beneath the load. And we think of Abraham and his son Isaac coming to a place of sacrifice. It's the same place; the very rock that's claimed to be the rock where Abraham offered up Isaac, it's only yards from the site of Calvary.

They go for it directly because time is of the essence and come to a small hill called Golgotha. There they crucify Him, which means they would have laid Jesus on that cross-piece, driven through each wrist in turn a great Roman nail, right at the head of the wrist, right through the central nerve as it runs down the arm. The pain would be unspeakable. Then, with some pulley arrangement, they would attach the cross-piece to the upright, fix it in place, and then the two feet, one on top of the other, another great nail driven again right through the central nerve down the leg and the foot. And He would be left there to die.

Hanging there in that position meant that the chest cavity was hugely constricted and so to open it to get breath, you had to pull and push and the pain would sear through the body and hands and feet. A gasp of breath and then you sink down again, and then another and another. That strange and terrible dance of death which was crucifixion, until eventually the victim, unable any longer to make the effort to breathe, would be mercifully delivered by asphyxiation. People hung on crosses sometimes for days, for a long, long time, and Jesus hung there. Such was crucifixion perfected by the Romans; so terrible that one Roman writer, Cicero, says a more cruel and terrible penalty it is impossible to describe.

There are four other little cameos round the cross. Other criminals on each side, Jesus in the midst, verse 18; appropriately to the very last He is among sinners. Then there's the business of the notice Pilate prepared: Jesus of Nazareth, King of the Jews. The high priests say,

'Change it!' 'What I've written, I've written.' Pilate will not be pushed any more. As one commentator rightly observes, he will not change the truth into a lie.

Then there are the clothes of Jesus; a belt, sandals, head turban, an outer garment, and an undergarment. The first four are quickly distributed but here's the fifth, rather special, seamless, woven in one piece top to bottom and so they gamble for it. You see an indication of God's presence even in the midst of all this darkness; a scripture from Psalm 22, a thousand years before is fulfilled astonishingly to the very letter: 'They divided My garments among them and cast lots for My clothing.' Then the further cameo, the four who cared; probably three women, including Jesus' mother, and John. 'A sword will pierce your soul,' Simeon had said. Now that sword was turning. What pain for Mary, for any mother to be there; and yet, where else should she be? She's there for Him. And Jesus ministers to her in His infinite love. 'Here's your son; here's your mother.'

He writhes on in the darkness; because darkness falls upon the whole land, terrible minute upon terrible minute, hour after hour. This is the king, the strangest king, an antithesis of every sense of dominion. He's also not just the strangest king but He is also the greatest king. 'Here is the King' is written in three languages. He claims the world. It's written in Greek, the language associated historically with the realm of culture. The church at times has turned a jaundiced eye upon all things artistic and creative but the world of culture is a world that Christ claims no less than any other. Human creativity surely is a gift of Him who made all things and these gifts, brought to His feet, can still be made a vehicle of His praise. 'Here is the King' is written in Latin, the language of government and law and institutions. Too often the church has appeared marginalised − unwilling to get involved in the often messy, sometimes evil world of business, politics and power, but Christ claims that world too as His own. He's able, through lives surrendered to His Lordship, to bring salt and light of His kingdom to the arenas of public life. And it's written in Hebrew, Aramaic, and Christ claims the world of religion which that language represents, also as His own. He alone is the truth, the way to God; He calls us to acknowledge Him and in His name to summon the lost millions, who follow the empty gods of other religious visions, to bow before this king, exalted on a cross. 'I, if I be lifted up, will draw people to Myself.'

One of the great limitations that has bedevilled the human saviours who, over the centuries have dreamed their great dreams and flung their empires around the world is that only too often in the process they lose sight of the individual. Our little personal universe of hope and pain and struggle and achievement is irrelevant to the great plan. The individual becomes expendable. Not so, this king. He rules in all the world and yet He also comes to us in our personal world; our King is the King of the world.

The death of Jesus (verses 28–30)

We come to the last moments of Jesus' life. 'I thirst,' He cries, knowing as He does that everything is now complete. 'It is finished, it is all accomplished; I'm thirsty.' A drink is given. Having received the drink, He said, verse 30, 'It is finished.' With that He bowed His head and gave up His spirit. To the last He retains the initiative; He gives up Himself. 'No one takes my life from me,' He said. 'I lay it down.' And so He does, for us.

What shall we say of this great statement, 'It is finished'? What is finished? His obedience to His Father's will for one thing is finished. 'My meat,' He said, 'is to do the will of Him who sent Me and to finish His work.' Now it is finished, the Lamb is spotless to the last. Obedience to His Father's will is finished, His casting out of His Father's enemy is finished. In His death He drives the cross through the heart of Satan and there it remains.

Thirdly, the revealing of His Father's heart is finished. He had said, 'Whoever sees Me, sees the Father.' In His prayer: 'I have revealed You to those You've given Me.' Here is that revelation in its climactic expression. Here we see how holy God is. We come to the cross and realise God cannot overlook sin. He can't ignore it. He can't forget it. He can't turn away from it as if it never happened. Sin matters. I see at the cross, as you see, what sin does to God. How holy God is, but oh, how loving God is. We need to come back and back to the cross and affirm that.

We live in a world of tragedy, sorrow, darkness, and sometimes we wonder why is God silent? God is not silent. He speaks at the cross across all the ages, the word comes down in every generation. It thunders forth from Calvary; God is love. And that is God on the cross. There is no God behind the back of Jesus. That is God into the infinite depths of the eternal depths of His being; He is the God of Calvary, He's the God of the cross, He's the God of infinite everlasting love. Look at the cross and say this to yourself: that is not just what God thought about me two thousand years ago ... that is exactly how God thinks of me and feels about me right now.

Finally, the redeeming of the Father's world is finished at the cross. There are various options of interpretation and time would allow me to comment on perhaps one of them. The note that John provides verses 14 and 36 links all this to the events taking place in Jerusalem around that very time – the Passover. That feast in remembrance of that moment down in Egypt, when for the liberation of the people of God, the spotless lamb was slain. Now all these centuries later, the perfect Lamb of God is slain upon the altar and His blood is shed that we might be set free. Jesus takes the cup and it's appropriate in a sense that the whole thing ends at that point. 'I am thirsty', and they gave Him a drink and verse 30 says 'When He had received the drink. [He] said, "It is finished."' Surely in a sense another hand is holding out another cup – He takes that cup, a cup of wrath, a cup of judgement, from the hand of His Father. He drinks it to the final dregs and He holds it upside down and not another drop runs out. 'It is finished.' Salvation, full and free, for all His people, for ever more. Hallelujah, what a Saviour.

So we come to that cross, we take that finished work of Christ and we know that our righteousness is complete in Him. We know that there is nothing more for us to do, blessed be God. We know, with Wesley

No condemnation now I dread,
Jesus and all in Him is mine.
Alive in Him, my living head,
and clothed in righteousness divine.
Bold, I approach the eternal throne
and claim the crown through Christ my own.

The piercing of His side (verses 31–37)

Two remaining moments, I just touch them. Jesus and the others are
hanging on the cross and it's Passover time. They've got to have them
down and so they ask for the application of the breaking of the legs
of the crucified which ended things because they could no longer
push up and breathe, and so quickly expired. They apply it to the two
others, but in Jesus' case, He's already dead. To make absolutely sure,
they transfix Him with a Roman spear.

Let's be absolutely clear – Jesus was dead. I say that simply
because this swoon theory still percolates around. It's standard
Islamic apologetic and it's absolute nonsense. Of course He was
dead. Romans killed people all the time. That same spear had probably been thrust through dozens before Jesus. Besides which, how
could He, having barely escaping death, a few days later have filled
the disciples with a radiant conviction that He'd not only come
back but He'd conquered death. The thing's impossible. He was
dead.

The blood pours. But there's something else – water. Because
He died probably of cardiac arrest, as the final act of taking
the world's sin upon Him, that ultimate trauma, there is a gathering of fluid around the lungs, pericardial effusion around the
heart, and so the water flows out. John sees it and knows it's
water, the great symbol of the Spirit, the water of life. Jesus talked
to Nicodemus about it. He talked to the woman of Samaria. He
spoke of the Spirit that they would receive and so wonderfully,
even as Jesus dies, the Spirit is stirring. These marvellous prophecies are fulfilled, from Exodus, and Zechariah, and the Psalms.

We're talking five hundred years before for Zechariah, a thousand years before for the Psalms, thirteen hundred years before in Exodus, fulfilled to the letter. God's in control; the Spirit is moving.

The burial of Jesus (verses 38–42)

Nicodemus and Joseph, these secret disciples, are suddenly brought out into the open, and come out for Christ, the forerunners of that great host around the world across the ages who would come forth boldly in the name and for the sake of Jesus. Of the spices they wrap around Him, seventy-five pounds of them (verse 39), we're told that the only others who ever had that much spice were kings. So at the place where Jesus was crucified, there was a garden; and in the garden a new tomb in which no one had ever been laid, and because it was the Jewish day of Preparation, and since the tomb was nearby, they laid Jesus there.

I finish with two things simply, first some Scripture, and the other from hymnody

> Let your attitude be the one you have through union with Christ Jesus who, though He was God, He did not demand or cling to His rights as God; He made Himself nothing. He took the humble position of a slave, and appeared in human form, and in human form He obediently humbled Himself even further by dying a criminal's death on a cross.
>
> (Phil. 2:5-8)

And the hymn:

> My song is love unknown;
> my Saviour's love to me;
> love to the loveless show,
> that they might lovely be.
> Oh who am I, that for my sake,
> my Lord should take frail flesh and die?

He came from His blest throne
salvation to bestow,
but men made strange and none
the longed-for Christ would know.
But O my friend! my friend indeed,
who at my need His life did spend.

Sometimes they strew His way,
and His sweet praises sing,
resounding all the day,
hosannas to their King.
Then Crucify! is all their breath,
and for His death they thirst and cry.

They rise and needs will have
my dear Lord made away;
a murderer they save;
the prince of life they slay.
Yet cheerful He to suffering goes,
That He His foes from thence might free.

In life, no house, no home
My Lord on earth might have;
in death no friendly tomb,
but what a stranger gave.
What may I say? Heav'n was His home;
but mine the tomb wherein He lay.

Here might I stay and sing,
no story so divine;
never was love dear king,
never was grief like thine.
This is my friend, in whose sweet praise
I all my days would gladly spend.

                                        Samuel Crossman 1624-83

Resurrection
Chapter 20: 1 – 31

Introduction

I want to divide this into three parts. 'Resurrection – wow!' point one; 'Resurrection – what?', point two and 'Resurrection – so what?' is point three. I want to go through the chapter three times picking up under these heads and I hope you'll be comfortable with that.

Resurrection – wow!

That is the discovery of the resurrection of Jesus. It's Sunday, very early, still dark and that summarises where the disciples are at this point. It's that day of the funeral kind of feeling … where we go through empty rituals and duties but there are no goals any more. Mary comes to the tomb. Not alone; it reads like that, a little, as you read it first time in John, but the other gospels make clear other women are with her. They discover the tomb open; the great stone that was rolled in front of the tomb has been rolled back. What's happened? Clearly they look in, or one of them does, and reports the body's gone, and there's panic. Is this the last twist of the knife on the part of the authorities? To take away His body? Or is it grave robbers?

Peter and John

They run to Peter. Despite his denials, he's still a respected leader. John comes and they run to the tomb. John, a younger man, by all accounts, wins the race. He bends and looks into the tomb (verse 5) but Peter, typically, blunders straight in. Both he and John see the grave clothes – the strips of linen lying there and also that burial cloth around His head, folded up by itself (verse 7) separate from the linen. Peter goes away wondering; John sees and believes. That's the usual word for 'faith' in the New Testament, so I take it to mean that he believes at the very least that Jesus is risen. Clearly the state of the tomb is what awakened that conviction. There's no sign of plunder here; this is not grave robbery. This is all peace and calm. Quite arguably the strips which would have been wound round the body, packed with these spices, are now lying still encircling and the head turban still entwined as if round Jesus' head. John Stott puts it like this: 'What John saw was like a discarded chrysalis from which the butterfly has emerged.' John had been at the tomb of Lazarus and he had seen Lazarus resuscitated. He was held by the grave clothes and they'd had to let him out, but Jesus has no grave clothes, He's clothed in His new humanity and He's not held back. John sees and wonder breaks upon him. This is not resuscitation! This is resurrection! He doesn't have a full faith about it yet (verse 9). He hasn't quite got to saying, 'But He had to rise!' That would come later. But he knows enough to believe.

Mary

Then we go back to Mary (verse 11) and she's crying outside the tomb. Think of what she'd been through in the last few hours – having been at the cross, and all the horror of that, then coming to the tomb to perform the final rites that Sunday morning, to mourn and continue with the work of embalming. Now that's taken from her. Even her blessed Lord, His body has been snatched away. Maybe there's anxiety in this woman's heart. Luke's gospel tells us she had been delivered by Jesus, demons had been cast from her, and now Jesus was gone. What was the prospect of retaining that new freedom? What about the possibilities of a re-invasion of the darkness?

She's a very distraught woman. She looks in and there are two angels. But even this vision of angels doesn't cure Mary. They ask her a question. 'Woman, why are you crying?' From the perspective of heaven, tears are so utterly inappropriate. If there's any time in history where tears are less appropriate, it's at the empty tomb of Jesus. It's a place for singing, dancing, celebration – and she's weeping. 'Why are you crying?' 'They've taken away my Lord … I don't know where they've put Him.' What a statement of desolation that is (verse 13). Then she turns round to Jesus but she doesn't recognise Him. She's so cocooned in her grief that she can't focus on Him. 'Why are you crying? Who is it you are looking for?' There's a clue there – who, not a body but a person. But she thinks He must be someone in charge here, the gardener maybe. 'If you've taken Him away, tell me where you've put Him. I'll go and get Him.' Then the moment of disclosure and it is so beautifully told. C.H. Dodd comments 'There is something indefinably first hand about this. There's nothing quite like it in the gospels.'

One word: 'Mary!' That remakes her world. She's running and embracing Him. Can we see here what Jesus talks about earlier in the gospel (chapter 5) of that day when those in the graves will hear the voice of the Son of God and those who are dead will come forth to life? I know about the intermediate state; we affirm it there in the sense of Jesus in His presence. But what we look forward to is this great day, the new heaven and earth of righteousness, the coming of the Lord when He will call us forth into resurrected life. It's a wonderful thought that what will call us will be our own name. He will call us as He called Mary.

Mary can't cling to Jesus. There are new dimensions for Him and must be also for her. It's got to be shared. 'Go, tell My brothers.' She's off, this radiant woman, the church's first evangelist: 'I have seen the Lord.'

The disciples

She comes to the disciples but then, she's a woman, so they don't believe. Here they are in this upper room, still locked in from fear of the Jews. Then the glory of Easter breaks upon them. Jesus comes and stands amongst them and says, 'Peace be with you.' He shows them His hands and His side. 'Touch Me. Handle Me! A ghost does not have flesh and blood as I have.' It's real, it's resurrection.

The disciples were overjoyed when they saw the Lord. Part of that joy in that moment surely was fed out of their experience of the temple liturgy, which is wonderfully reflected in the motion and action of Jesus. In the liturgy, that great day of atonement was the occasion, once every year, when the high priest would go into the Holy of Holies, behind the veil, to cast that blood upon the mercy seat to make atonement for all the people. All the courts would throng with worshippers, and at the high point of the worship the high priest would take the sacrifice and disappear from view behind the veil. A hush would come upon the people. Would the sacrifice be acceptable? Would God affirm them and express atonement for their sin? Then, after a pause, suddenly the curtain would tremble and the high priest would reappear and cry in his greeting, '*Shalom*! Peace!' Peace with God.

This great high priest offers on that cross His one full complete sufficient sacrifice in atonement for the sin of the world. He's buried, He's hidden and where is He? Is it accepted? Suddenly the curtain trembles and He's there among them. 'Peace! *Shalom*!' He showed them His hands and His side. Oh the wonder of it. Our sin – not in part but the whole – He has carried to the cross. That's part of the joy that was theirs and it's the joy that's ours as Christ meets us with those same words: 'Peace be with you.'

Thomas

Thomas wasn't there, but a week later he is (verse 26). Again the wonder of Easter as Jesus appears for Thomas. 'Look, here's My hands, here's My side; put your finger here, reach into My side, and stop doubting. Believe!' Thomas responds the only way you can respond to the reality of Easter. 'My Lord and my God.' Resurrection – wow!

Resurrection – what?

It's historical …

I want to say three things about this. First of all, the resurrection is historical. John understands this as an actual event – a specific location at a datable point in history. It's not a myth. The tomb is empty and so they can touch Him; fingers can be placed in His wounds. But there is something more than normal history here. This is the sovereign action of God breaking gloriously into history, so there's more than the normal historical experience, but not less.

… but it's more than history

Secondly: when we're asking what the nature of the resurrection is, the full assurance of Christ being raised goes beyond historical evidence. That's hinted at (verse 9). Here is John seeing the empty tomb, the grave clothes, coming to faith but the Scripture says he didn't yet understand from Scripture that Jesus had to rise from the dead. There was another dimension there beyond the historical evidence, the witness of the word – the inspired Scripture. Back in chapter 17, Jesus talked about giving His words to the disciples, that they might have certainty so the certainty came through receiving the words. Paul gives a good example of that where he says there 'our gospel came to you not simply with words, but also with power, with the Holy Spirit and with deep conviction'(1 Thess.1:5). The Greek word there means full persuasion.

Evidences

Thirdly, while John and the other evangelists are not setting out to prove the resurrection – they are more concerned with its implications theologically and personally – yet their accounts of the resurrection contain clear evidences that persuasively undergird the historicity of the resurrection. I'm being very alert to all the debates around this. He didn't write to prove it, but his presentation with the others give us evidences that significantly undergird the fact historically of Christ rising.

The empty tomb

What are these evidences? In this chapter there's the empty tomb (verses 1-9). Jesus' body has gone. It's virtually impossible to deny that. In a few days time, these same apostles bear witness to the resurrection in Jerusalem. When Peter stood on the day of Pentecost, he was no further away from the tomb of Jesus than I am, this morning, from the shores of Derwentwater. It was a matter of a few hundred yards. Peter was to preach at Pentecost, centraling his message on the resurrection, talking about David's tomb – 'which we have to this day' – by contrast, Jesus' tomb, we have also, but it's untenanted. How did they persuade them in Jerusalem of the reality of the resurrection – the central plank of their witness – unless that tomb was empty? Paul Althaus says, 'The resurrection could not have been maintained in Jerusalem for a single day, even for a single hour, if the emptiness of the tomb had not been established as a fact for all concerned.' These people were Jews and they didn't believe, like the Greeks believed, that the body lies a-mouldering in the grave and the soul goes marching on. For the Hebrew, the unity of the human person meant that resurrection meant a grave-emptying business.

The disciples' witness

Of course folks say 'The disciples stole the body.' Come on! There's this beautiful sincerity about the whole thing. These accounts are not fabricated. These disciples died for this thing, excruciatingly! There's not a hint anywhere in the succeeding years of any diminution of conviction, of any Passover plot they put together and had to hang desperately on to. They hadn't taken it.

The authorities

What about the authorities? As the disciples began to witness, embarrassingly successfully in Jerusalem, these authorities would have given anything for any evidence to deflate this whole movement. In Acts 4, Peter and John are before them and they want to stop this thing, and what do they say? The best they can come up with is 'Stop, OK!' Poor fools. If ever there was a company in history had access to all the evidence of where Jesus' body was, to point it out, or to give evidence of where it had been disposed, it was them! A far better position that any sceptical scholars in the twentieth/twenty-first century. Yet they do not come up with that evidence. Why? Because it wasn't there. It never was and never would be. Jesus was raised.

His appearances

We go on to some of His appearances; first to Mary, so authentic, then to these disciples and then to Thomas. There was no question about these things. Professor Jim Dunn in the University of Durham can say that it's virtually impossible to dispute that at the historical roots of Christianity lie experiences of the first Christians who understood them as appearnaces of Jesus raised by God from the dead. If hallucination will not fit the evidence and it doesn't, then again we've got to the same place. Christ is raised. Then there's the transformation of the disciples. How are these frightened sheep huddled in that room suddenly becoming these bold lions, taking on their whole nation in Acts chapter 2? Yes the Holy Spirit came, but it's evident that the transformation happened before that. The only thing that fits is the resurrection. How do you explain that transformation?

The church and the word

Then there's these other things; the existence of the church and the New Testament. If Jesus Christ was not raised from the dead you wouldn't be in Keswick, there'd be no convention, there'd be no Christian church for two thousand years to hand down the witness that this convention bears witness to. Another piece of evidence; have you got a Bible there? Reach to the middle of your Bible and divide off the Old Testament from the New Testament in your fingers. There would be none of that New Testament part in your fingers if Jesus was not raised from the dead.

Christ is risen and this is a day for dancing. G.K. Chesterton was once criticised by an agnostic friend for maintaining his Christian faith in the modern world. The argument was depressingly familiar: 'surely you can't hold to that kind of belief in this contemporary scientific world.' To which Chesterton replied, 'My good sir, far from disbelieving I'm actually prancing with belief!' We are prancing with belief, because Jesus is raised from the dead.

Resurrection – so what?

What follows from it? We can look at this under three heads: implications for ourselves, implications for the church, and implications for Jesus. We're going to take them in that order although that's the reverse order in which they occur in the chapter.

Implications for ourselves

We are those who have believed though we have not seen (verse 29). Because of that (verse 31) we have life in His name. The glorious implication that is being stated by John here as far as the resurrection is concerned for our lives personally is: we share the resurrection. If you're a Christian you have been planted in union with Christ in His death, and raised up with Him in new life. The resurrection life that flowed through Jesus is now flowing within us. We have been raised with Christ, as Paul puts it (Col. 3:1) and that by believing (verse 31).

Doubting Thomases

Believing is sometimes a little difficult and that's why I think we've been given this whole story of Thomas. There's nothing perfect in this world and faith itself is not always straightforward. Doubts arise for all of us at different times as they did for Thomas. It's something to bring into the open and not be ashamed about acknowledging. 'Lord, I believe, help my unbelief!' is the cry of the Christian heart at times.

It can be agonising. Remember Job in the midst of his suffering, crying out in the 23rd chapter, 'If only I knew where to find Him!' We cry with Mary in verse 13, 'They have taken my Lord away and I don't know where they have put Him.' I remember in my early twenties, eighteen months when I lived a Christian life without any sense of God whatever. That was challenging because I was very involved in intervarsity UCCF at the time, I was given leadership in my own university, and nationally. I still said my prayers, read the Bible, attended church. But I had absolutely no sense of the reality of God, Jesus and the Spirit, all of that was gone. God gradually by His mercy brought me out of that. I have great sympathy with all the Thomases. Thomas helps us understand some of these experiences because he is a good type of the doubter.

Of course you can build too much on these New Testament biographies. We don't get a lot of information about these apostles but Thomas appears in chapter 11, saying that he is ready to go to Jerusalem and die with Jesus, and in chapter 14 he's the spokesperson for those who haven't grasped even the basic content of Jesus going away to the Father and then we meet Him here. Not a lot to build on but he was rather an imaginative person who liked only what he's sure of. No bad quality in itself but folk like that sometimes won't dare allow themselves to dream at all and they're very limited by their immediate experience. We don't deserve to go to heaven, and we wonder and are open to periods of doubt. Then there is also isolation, that has to be said is a contributive factor. Jesus met the disciples, but Thomas wasn't there. Perhaps, true to his temperament, he was the kind of guy that had to be alone after the crucifixion, work it all out in his mind but he missed out on the meeting.

As a preacher, I want to tell you, on behalf of my fellow preachers, we do not compose sermons for particular people. That's not the aim; we seek a word from God. But again and again as you prepare a message, you sometimes get a wonderful sense of who this is going to be wonderfully helpful for. You go into the pulpit on a Sunday, rejoicing in anticipation in the way they're going to be blessed by this message and you look out from the pulpit and the pew is empty. It's not only discouraging for the preacher, it's devastating to the disciple. How many messages that God had ready to bless you with and you weren't there. I know we can't always be there every week but sometimes the reasons we're not there are trivial. We need to be like Thomas as he learned his lesson on that second weekend. Even though he's struggling with all kinds of doubts and they're infuriating him with their easy certainties, he's there and Jesus comes and he goes away blessed. Don't forsake the assembling of yourselves together.

Look beyond

Contradiction is perhaps the other thing; for Thomas there was this awful reality. Jesus had died, he saw the wounds. He couldn't get past it. People are like that. Not long ago, a woman said to me, 'I don't talk to God.' 'Why not?' 'I said to Him, if my mother dies I won't speak to You again. I've kept my promise.' That was years before, her mother was in her eighties, we don't have eternal life here! People get something in their minds and it blots everything else out. That was so with Thomas. We've got to learn to look beyond. Yes, there are tragedies, there are deep mysteries that all of us have to handle in our lives but we don't let these dominate. So for various reasons, Thomas struggles. But there are faith sources as well here and that's so encouraging. Look, negatively, it wasn't vision that made the difference. Or it won't make it for us, because we are those who have not seen and yet believe (verse 29). We don't look for visions, but what do we have? Like Thomas, we have the witness of those who saw Jesus, the apostles. That witness is included and incorporated in the Scriptures and so there's where we start, with God's word.

Jesus was there for Thomas. You say to me, 'Isn't it a little bit emotional, this personal encounter stuff?' It's not emotional. This is logic. If Jesus rose from the dead, then that means He's alive always. Death can't hold Him. If He's alive always, He's alive in 2002, here and now, and we can meet Him. I don't think that's emotion. I think that's logic. Thomas meets with Him, his doubts are addressed. Christ meets us at the point of our need as we trust and reach out to Him. Then there is that command at the end: 'Stop doubting and believe.' Sometimes we need to hear that summons to believe.

G.K. Chesterton talked about doubts about doubt. We need to doubt our doubts. Believe our beliefs, cast ourselves on to Christ and discover His reality and the renewal of faith. Then the summit of faith as Thomas makes the marvellous confession: 'My Lord and my God.' This in a way completes the gospel of John. It began with the confession of the apostle 'In the beginning was the Word, and the Word was with God'. Now here is a sinner saying, 'My Lord and my God.' A doubter is the one who crowns the gospel of belief.

Resurrection and the community

What does this resurrection mean as far as the community is concerned (verses 19-23)? Notice two things about the mission. 'As the Father has sent Me, I am sending you.' It's a mission patterned on the mission of Jesus. Resurrection inevitably leads to mission. Notice it's the same day. Jesus doesn't even give them any hours to reflect on the glory of the resurrection. He's already indicating that they've got to go for Him. It's a mission of the One who became incarnate and our mission needs equally to be incarnated in the world – including the world of hunger. Jesus' ministry cared for the hungry, feeding the five thousand. 20 per cent of our world hungry, 8 per cent starving, sixty thousand dying a day, forty thousand of them children. Then sickness; Jesus ministered to the sick. Think of HIV/AIDS. The figures are staggering. The deaths from AIDS are now about as many as died in all the wars in the twentieth century. HIV/AIDS is ravaging sub-Saharan Africa. In South Africa, 22 per cent of the population are thought to be infected. Up in Botswana it's 40 per cent. Just apply that to your community ... That's what they're facing and there's such disproportionate distribution of resources and medicines.

What about the ignorant? There are one billion people in our world with no access to real education. Then there's the most deprived people group on this planet, those who have never heard of Jesus, the unevangelised. About two billion because of the walls of culture and prejudice. Ten thousand people groups of our world with no viable church. Jesus speaks about this particularly in verse 23 when He talks about forgiving ... those who you forgive are forgiven, those who you don't forgive are not forgiven – He's surely talking about the witness to the gospel and this is part of what Easter means as it's applied to us.

There are resources. Verse 22, 'receive the Holy Spirit', and He breathed on them when He said that. Here's the great resource. People debate the relation between this and Pentecost. I think Jesus is teaching them something here. This is Pentecost in the sense of it preparing them for that great gift. What is the gift? What is the Holy Spirit? He is the breath of the risen Jesus, the life of the risen Lord flowing into our lives and enabling us for all the demands of mission.

The implications of the resurrection for Jesus

Verse 9 speaks of the larger dimensions of the whole biblical witness to the resurrection, which links it to the coming of the kingdom of God and all the prophetic writings that anticipated that. But as far as Jesus Himself is concerned, verse 17 is the key: 'Don't hold on to me, for I've not returned to the Father. But go instead to My brothers and tell them I'm returning' – 'I'm ascending' is a better translation, 'to My Father and Your Father, My God and Your God.' Resurrection is a moment in the movement of exaltation for Jesus, He's on His way to the right hand of the Father and so, because the tomb is empty, the throne is occupied. Jesus is Lord. That is His witness. 'All authority,' He can say, 'is given to Me in heaven and earth.' The early church bore witness to that with joy. Peter at Pentecost says: 'God has made this Jesus, whom you crucified, both Lord and Christ.' Stephen, as he died, is given the vision of the Son of Man standing at the right hand of God. That is the Jesus we meet and worship. Not the One who will be Lord one day; though that is wonderfully true, we will see Him on His throne when He returns; but One who is already exalted at God's right hand. Let me give you two illustrations of this as I finish.

Polycarp of Smyrna

Here in the year 160 we're in the city of Smyrna, under the pro-consulship of Statius Quadratus. The aged Polycarp, the bishop and saint of that church, is brought to trial during a local persecution. He's called upon to curse the name of Christ and he makes this marvellous reply, 'Fourscore and six years have I served Him and He never did me wrong. How then can I revile my King, my Saviour?' So they burned him to death in the amphitheatre. But the young church in Smyrna hurled its defiance in the very face of its murderers for when it later came to write down in the annals of the church where it happened, it was very careful to enter the precise date and it gave it thus: 'Polycarp was murdered. Statius Quadratus being pro-consul in Asia and Jesus Christ being King forever.' That's the faith. He is Lord.

Murder in the Cathedral

The spirit of it is caught so beautifully by T.S. Eliot in his play *Murder in the Cathedral*. As the priests bar the door of the great church of Canterbury against the would-be assassins, Thomas the archbishop, knowing they have done it for his safety, will not permit it. 'Unbar the doors!' he says. 'Throw open the doors. I will not have the house of prayer, the church of Christ, the sanctuary, turned into a fortress. The church shall be open, even to our enemies.' The priests protest, they are desperate. They say, 'You would bar the door against the lion, the leopard, the wolf or the boar, why not more against beasts with the souls of damned men and against men who damn themselves to beasts, my lord, my lord?' His answer rings out clear. 'We have fought the beast and have conquered – now is the triumph of the cross. Now open the door, I command it!'

That is the faith. He has conquered. He is Lord. In His name we go to the world. There is the wow of Easter! He is risen. Here is the 'what' – it's historically verified, it's true. There is the 'so what'; for ourselves individually, we share His risen life, for our church corporately – we go in mission to the world, for Jesus personally, He is Lord of all. Christ is risen – hallelujah!

Mission
Chapter 21:1 – 25

Introduction

We have been attempting to retell the heart of the greatest story ever told. We've been there with Jesus in His prayer of intercession, His arrest, His trials, His crucifixion, and His resurrection. Now we come to chapter 21.

There are two great questions that all preaching needs to answer. The first question is 'what', the exegetical question, what is the text saying and what is its meaning? Preaching has to go on to a second question, 'So what'? Chapter 21 is John's 'So what'? There is the glory of our Lord, His coming, His death, His rising, so what? It can be summed up in one word: mission.

The text that we can work from is back in chapter 20, verse 21: 'As the Father has sent me, I am sending you'. That has an earlier form, in the prayer of Jesus, 'As the Father sent Me into the world, I am sending you into the world' (Jn. 17:18). One of the things we need to grasp about mission is its sheer centrality. As you go through this gospel of John, mission is its theme from the beginning. The mission of the Son sent into the world by the Father dominates the whole first part of the gospel. But as that moves towards its climax, we begin to discover that there's another phase of mission that begins to develop out of that first phase of mission; the mission of the church, the apostles. When you look into this gospel you find again and again that the Father and Son are defined in terms of mission. The Father is the one who sent the Son; the Son is the one who has been sent by the Father, so mission defines the very character of God in His Trinity within this gospel. The gospel of John is the greatest book on mission ever written. It is its pervasive theme, the mission of the Son sent by the Father and out of that, the church sent by the Son.

The linkage of the two is critical and the tense of the verbs back in verse 21 of chapter 20 makes the point that the sender continues to be present, the animating force of the mission of the sent. As in the case of our Lord, sent by the Father, it's not that the Father leaves the Son and departs from the scene; rather, the whole mission of Jesus is the mission of the Father in and through Him. In the same way, the mission of the church, sent into the world by the Son, is the mission of Jesus continued through His people. It's not two missions, it's one great mission. One text says that unambiguously; Matthew 28, the great commission text. 'Go and make disciples of all the nations,' says Jesus, 'and I am with you.' Often we misrepresent that a little, we make it the comforting presence of Christ. In that context 'I am with you' means 'it's My mission and I'm inviting you to join Me'. Jesus is saying, 'go into all the world and make disciples. I'm going to do it, all authority in heaven and earth is Mine – are you coming with Me?' That is the nature of mission. Here is our Lord, risen from the dead and now He's sending us. In effect He's saying, 'I'm going to the world', the world that we return to – that church, that community, that workplace, that factory, that home, that school, that college, that neighbourhood, that family, that situation that we go back to. There, says Jesus, 'I'm going to work, and I invite you to come and join Me.'

Fishing with Jesus – verses 1-14

We begin at the Sea of Galilee. Seven of the disciples are going fishing. They fish at night and the shoals elude them and they've nothing to show for a whole night's fishing. What are they doing, fishing? Jesus is risen from the dead! What are they doing up in Galilee? They should be down in Jerusalem, waiting for the Spirit.

There are, however, some very good reasons why this is appropriate. First of all, Jesus had told them to go to Galilee, Matthew 28:10. Secondly, psychologically, this is exactly what any doctor would have ordered. Think of the emotional roller-coaster these men had been through in the last few days; Palm Sunday – hallelujah, hosanna, cheering, everything's great, Jesus is going to be accepted as Messiah, and then Thursday night, what's up? Then Friday, the cross, crucified, buried. Then Easter, He's alive! The best thing for them would surely be a night's fishing. As George Beasley Murray notes, 'though Jesus be risen from the dead, the disciples must still eat.' They fish in order to get food. Let's defend them.

The stranger on the shore

They've caught nothing but there's this stranger on the shore. Fishermen do not readily take advice, especially from someone on land. His call to them is quite colloquial – 'Hey lads,' He's almost saying, 'nothing last night, eh? Give it another go, on the right hand side.' The catch is incredible, they can hardly get it aboard. John, always intuitive, says 'It's the Lord. It's Jesus.' They come to land and Jesus has prepared a breakfast on the beach and they share it together. Suddenly we begin to get the meaning of all this, because fishing was the whole term in which He had called them at the first. 'Follow Me and I will make you fishers of men', Mark 1:17 or Luke 5. Fishing has been the way they've seen their mission with Jesus up to this point and so here we are moving on to a new phase of it. Jesus is bringing them back to that so that He might re-commission them for what lies ahead.

There are two factors I want to note in terms of the context of this. First there's the general context; this is taking place in Galilee. I don't know what you think about Galilee. When I was a kid I always thought Galilee was a very sleepy, backwoods town. Nothing ever happened. That was where Jesus was brought up, a nice quiet place.

The historians have exploded that. Galilee was a place of huge stir and movement, on the edge of one of the great trade routes of the world. Trade and people moved and in terms of population, if Josephus' figures are right, the Galilee region was probably, at that point, the most densely populated area of the world! That is where our Lord was moulded, in the midst of a clash of cultures, civilisations and ideas that swept through the world of the time.

He takes them back to Galilee because His call to them is to the wider world out there, beyond Israel to the world. He takes them to the edge of this great Gentile world because that is where primarily their mission's going to be. The other reason for the location is that He brings them back to where it all began. What He's saying is, 'I called you three years ago; now things have changed. You know as never before what this business of being with Me is going to cost you, you know your own limitations and weaknesses. The easy idealism, that's gone; and you know the message more clearly. There's the promise of the Spirit to enable you, but now we enter upon the next phase. I want to know – are you still with Me, as I make My way into the nations and the ends of the earth? Will you now follow Me?'

Notice how that 'Follow Me' echoes the early chapters of John and the other calling accounts in the other gospels. I think that is the whole point of this incident and that relates to where we are this morning. We're all facing new chapters in our lives. The world is facing a new chapter. It's rather threatening, we don't want to think about it very much. Who knows what the next year's going to bring? Many of us are standing on the edge of something new. Jesus meets us and He's saying to us, 'Can I count on you now?'

He takes us back to that place of earlier commitment. I don't know what your equivalent of that shoreline in Galilee is, a place of your conversion or your confirmation or your baptism, a place of dedication or some moment when God met you with His Spirit, a moment in desperation when you cried out to the Lord and you said, 'If You'll do this, I will give my life to You.' The Lord's taking us back there. He's saying, 'Do you still stand behind that commitment? Are you ready to follow Me?'

Following Jesus – verses 15–23

All that this chapter does is tease out what following Jesus implies. You've heard about the three Rs of education. Let me give you the six Rs of mission.

Reliance

That's the whole point of this fishing exercise. There's a stark contrast between fishing undertaken at the behest of the disciples on the basis of their own experience and fishing undertaken under the leadership of Jesus. In the one case nothing, in the other case an overwhelming catch. As one applies this to the world of mission, one cannot but see some parallels here to the contrast between mission experienced in the industrialised world, and mission experienced in the developing world. Here is just one statistic. There's a city near us in western Canada, Calgary. There was a very good study done a few years ago of evangelism in the evangelical churches of Calgary, to establish how many real outsiders these churches were winning to Christ. You know what they came up with? 1.9 per year – less than two people. I don't think Calgary's untypical. Then you go to the third world, what a difference. Let me give one instance.

Up in the central highland area of Cameroon, some of the Baptist folk there had had a real problem, a few years ago. The churches were mushrooming, springing up everywhere, but they'd no leadership. They were very concerned and so they sought the Lord's face. They'd established a number that they wanted to aim for, people who would be leaders, and they would train them. So they sought the Lord and He laid His hands on people and sure enough, wonderfully, they met their target. Then they discovered that no sooner had they got them trained, the problem was as big as ever. Because in the meantime there were all these other churches springing up and they were still at the bottom of the hill. Which country in the western world has problems like that, regularly?

George Hoffman, the first director of Tearfund, put it very beautifully. He'd spent a few days with a tribe in quite a remote part of Uganda, a Christian tribe. During his few days with them he was absolutely astonished because these people had nothing. They had almost no food and yet strangely they always seemed to be able to eat. When they got sick they all prayed and people got healed. There were bandits in the area and danger and yet they always seemed to know how to escape. After a few days, George came to one of the elders of the tribe and said, 'I can't understand this. These things don't seem to happen in the west.' The elder very wisely said to him, 'George, in the west you have God and things. Here in Africa we just have God.'

We can't become like that. The toothpaste can't go back in the tube. We have all these technological helps and applications from all kinds of sciences. We thank God for this, it's helpful. The deadly danger is that we trust in them and then we no longer need to trust in God. The index of how much we trust in God is very simple. How much do we pray? You can't evade the challenge of that. If we pray it's because we have to, because we depend on God; but if we don't pray much, we feel we can get by without Him.

In Seoul, Korea, the churches there are at prayer almost all the time. I went to Yongghi Cho's church, to the prayer meeting. It was the whole night. I discovered that one or two other folk had decided to turn up too, twenty-five thousand of them. God blesses. There's a principle here. I think part of our problem is that we make our targets too easy to hit. We set our targets for our church, reaching our community, reaching our world, we put the target about two feet away. Then we get our arrow, woof, right in the centre!

See what God does to these disciples? He picks up the target and carries it five miles down the road. He says: 'You reach the world!' This handful of nobodies? What else can they do – they fall on their knees, they pray, they pray and they pray. What happens? Do you need me to tell you? Suddenly there's a sound from heaven like the rush of a mighty wind. Yes, I know, Pentecost is unique and all that – let's go into Acts 4 if we don't like Acts 2. Here they are gathered together and now they're threatened with persecution, and suddenly as they pray the place is shaken. When did that last happen in our prayer meetings? They needed it, they were desperate – the target was so far down the road. They had to get God on their side! Maybe the Lord would like us to move our targets back a bit. Then we'd start to pray and we'd rely on Him and then this little story in John 21 might come alive in our church and in our lives.

Repentance

Peter is being re-commissioned (verses 15-17). He's getting stuff dealt with. It's difficult not to make the connection; after all, Jesus builds this fire. When was the last time Peter warmed himself at a fire? And threefold questioning ... As Westcott says, it's irresistible once you see the connection; the threefold denial. I know Luke says there was an appearance to Peter probably prior to this and so the stuff had started to get sorted out, but it seems there's more to do, and Peter is being called here to reaffirm his faith and to get that threefold denial out of his life. Peter is getting forgiven, and then moving on.

I am so anxious that we all should get to that place of being forgiven and moving on. Isn't it true in all our lives that most of us have two lists of sins? We've got list number A, the respectable list. You know, it's the sins we wouldn't mind sharing. They're Christian sins. We come to the Lord asking forgiveness and the Lord forgives us and that's fine, they're all dealt with. I think many of us have got another list, List B. List B is buried in our hearts and we would be totally embarrassed for that list to be read in a public place. They're the sins that never get dealt with. We keep on clearing off List A. List B lingers. Part of the reason is because of pride. Something inside ourselves is saying, I never did these things. Me, the spiritual leader, this mature Christian? So we don't face them. The second thing about these sins – we're not bringing them to the Lord because we feel the Lord would be embarrassed with these things. That takes me to the third thing – we need to come to Christ with these things and realise Christ died for sinners: while we were still sinners in all the darkness and the filth and the degradation, whatever it is, that's where His blood reaches. By hanging on to these, we're reducing Jesus. We're saying He's only a bit Saviour. He can deal with List A but He can't deal with List B. We're dishonouring Him. We need to come to Christ and make Him a total Saviour. We let God be God, and therefore we let Christ deal with these things too, and we add to His magnificence and His greatness and His grace by letting Him deal with these List B things in our lives. Look at Him on that cross. Isn't it amazing, the wonder of His love for us, doing all that for us: is He not able to forgive all our sins? Let's take that List B out of the back of our hearts, let's tear it up in His presence right now in our minds and throw it away into the depths of God's forgetfulness.

Peter is re-commissioned. Christ doesn't just deal with the negative but He gives us a positive in its place; Peter is given his role and a ministry back. Peter Snowden says it very well: 'If you ask me what forgiveness means, it's the wonder of being trusted again by God in the place where I disgraced Him.' Notice this is all public. It's happening around the other disciples. God has great work for Peter to do publicly, but it won't work if Peter's under the shadow as the guy that denied Jesus. Jesus is refurbishing Peter's public image. There's a great lesson for all of us who are in Christian ministry/Christian leadership: you can trust God with your public image. I struggled to learn it; we all tend to be so sensitive to how we're being perceived and we want to make sure we get a little polish and our proper place. I think in this passage God says, 'Relax!' The Lord knows exactly how much publicity, how much affirmation we need. We can trust Him with that.

Responsibility

What does Jesus say to Peter? He says 'Feed My lambs, feed My sheep.' Notice they're all verbs. We like nouns – 'I am a shepherd.' Jesus says, 'Feed My sheep. ' We qualify as servants by serving, it's by doing. Never mind what we are, it's what we do – that's ministry. Notice that it's Christ's lambs and sheep. We ministers sometimes fall into bad habits – 'My church. My people, my congregation.' No! They're never ours. They're His. Peter didn't forget that and when he wrote his letter, he said 'Tend the flock of God that is under your care.' Despite all the difficulties of these sheep – and some of them will drive you insane – they're still His. They're not ours. We get a temporary opportunity to be an under-shepherd.

Notice further that the lambs and sheep matter to Jesus? Let me illustrate that in this way. Here's Peter Maiden here, and let's suppose, for the sake of my illustration, Peter and I have been friends for many years. We went through college together, we've been partners in ministry for a while, but during all that time we never thought about women at all. Never thought about getting married – it never crossed our minds. Peter weakens and he meets Win and they get married. I go round for a first visit to their home, after their honeymoon, eager to tell him what's been happening. I press the bell, the door opens, Win lets me in, I take off my coat, throw it over her, and I get inside, sit down with Peter and we're talking away and then the meal. We go down to the table and there's this beautiful meal that Win's made, oh, it's so superb but I've not had a thought for that, I'm talking to Peter about the times we shared and the things we've had. Sooner or later and probably sooner rather than later, Peter will hold up his hand and say, 'Bruce! We've had great friendship over the years and that's great and we've shared tremendous stuff together but you need to know, I'm no longer a single guy. I've got a wife, I married Win, and she's here, and I want you to know I've been hurt tonight. You threw your coat over her, and then we sit down at this marvellous meal, she's spent hours preparing it. You've not acknowledged it, you've not appreciated it. All the time you're talking to me, you don't talk to her, you're not bringing her into the conversation, but I want you to know: I love this woman. She's my wife, I care about her. If you want to relate to me from now on, you've got to include her, because I love her, she's my wife.'

Do I need to make the application? It's simple. Jesus Christ is married. He has a bride. It's the church and this rapping with Jesus has to embrace His bride about whom He cares. Does He care? Oh yes. Christ loved the church and gave Himself for her. We need to learn to be lovers of the church if we are to love Jesus.

Rigour

That's the word for cost – but I had to get another R. It's in verse 18. Another great principle; mission involves rigour, cost. Two things: loss of control. Notice, Henry Nouwen says some quite profound things around this

The world says when you were young you were dependent and could not go where you wanted, but when you are old you will be able to make your own decisions, go your own way and control your own destiny but Jesus has a different vision of maturity. It is the ability and willingness to be led where you would rather not go. Immediately after Peter has been re-commissioned to be a leader of His sheep, Jesus confronts him with the hard truth that the servant leader is the leader who is being led to unknown, undesirable and painful places. The way of the Christian leader is not the way of upward mobility but of downward mobility, ending on the cross.

That's echoed by some words of Oswald Chambers, 'I am called to live in relationship to God so that my life produces a longing after God in other lives, not admiration for myself. This is hard but it's true. God is not after perfecting me to be a specimen in His showroom. He is after getting me to the place where He can use me.' That's what Jesus is talking about, losing control – He is Lord.

Part of the cost is also loss of life, because stretching out your hand is a euphemism for crucifixion. Jesus is prophesying Peter's own crucifixion, his loss of life, his martyrdom and in our world today that resonates. We are at the moment functioning with martyrdoms of around sixty-eight thousand a year which is pretty well par for the past one hundred years. It's responsibly computed by David Barrett, that one in two hundred Christians alive in the world today will die as martyrs. That's the world we're in but it is the way the Master went, should not the servant tread it still – do we complain? He gave His all for us and this is following Jesus. If necessary, we give all for Him. Samuel Rutherford said a profound word of his generation but it resonates for ours: 'God has called us to Christ's side, and the wind is now in Christ's face in this land. And seeing you are with Him, you cannot expect the sheltered or the sunny side of the hill.'

Relationships

Peter turns and sees this disciple, John, following (verses 20-22). Peter's got his own future spelled out and he's had a nice time with Jesus, he's in with the Lord. 'Lord, what about him?' Bishop Taylor Smith, a great supporter of this convention in earlier years, wrote in the margin of his Bible beside these words, 'Mind your own business'! That's exactly what Jesus says! 'What is that to you? You follow Me!' Peter's got to come to terms with the fact of diversity in Christian life in gifting and ministry. Peter would be the preacher, John would be the penman. Peter would be the shepherd, John, the seer. Peter the foundational witness, John the faithful writer. Peter would die in the agony of martyrdom, John would live on to a great age and pass away in serenity; the reality of partnership in following Jesus. There are many others on the road with us, as truly Christ's, as surely commissioned, as deeply loved, as greatly valued; their calling and gifts are different from ours. Their instincts, even their convictions on certain matters, may not coincide with ours, but we can thank God for them and at times be inspired, challenged, by their example. In the end, however, the focus is on Jesus. 'You must follow Me.'

When I became a Christian, my dad gave me a piece of advice that was the only piece of advice he gave me as a Christian. He said, 'Bruce, take your Christianity from Christ and not from other Christians.' I thank God for other Christians, they've been wonderful for me, they've kept me right again and again, I bless God for them, but that's been a great help to me over the years. Follow Jesus.

Return

Here is the ultimate parameter of mission (verses 22,23). This is where it all leads, this is where it will all end. 'The church,' says Lesslie Newbiggin, 'is the pilgrim people of God on the move, hastening to the ends of the earth to beseech all people to be reconciled to God, and hastening to the end of time to meet its Lord Who will gather all into one.' His return – how we anticipate it; that He Who died in shame on that cross and rose again gloriously on the third day, Who is with us, the living Lord, through His Spirit right now and walks and talks with us through our Christian life and service, that He will come. He's on His way, and right down the long avenue of the future you can see Him and every day He's coming closer until that day, and it may not be far off, when He beats upon the great doors of time, and the doors swing wide to admit Him, and we'll see Him on His throne and we'll crown Him Lord of all. Jesus' prayer, back in John chapter 17 verse 24 will be fulfilled. 'I pray that they may see my glory,' That makes it all so utterly worthwhile. 'Be steadfast therefore,' says Paul, 'in the Lord's mission and service. Immovable, abound in God's work.' Why? 'Because you know that your work is not in vain in the Lord.' Or, as J.B. Phillips puts it very appropriately, 'Know that nothing you ever do for Him is lost or wasted. It will be worth it all when we see Jesus.' It will be worth it all when we see Him, His glorious return and until then, we give ourselves to follow Him. Reliance upon Him, repentance of our sin, accepting responsibility for His people, facing the rigour and the cost of mission, engaging in relationships with others for His sake, and anticipating His return.

Visions of God
Themes from Ezekiel

by Liam Goligher

LIAM GOLIGHER

Converted at an early age, Liam felt a strong call to preach at the age of twelve, primarily through the showing of a Billy Graham film. He started preaching to cows and graduated to people at the age of fifteen. After studying in Belfast, he pastored churches in Ireland, Canada and his native Scotland. Outside the local church, he has been involved in student ministry in the UK and eastern Europe. Since 2000, he has been Senior Minister of Duke Street Church in Richmond. With five children, Liam's main recreational activity is that of taxi driver. Any spare time he does have, he likes to use for swimming, fishing, walking the dog or going to the movies.

Vision Express
Chapter 1:1 – 3:15

Introduction

Some birthdays are more memorable than others. One of the things I've discovered is – since moving down to a part of London where the majority of the population is in its mid-twenties through to its late-thirties – thirty has become the significant birthday. I recently came across some of the symptoms of those who are heading towards that crucial moment in their lives. How do you know when you are about to turn thirty?

- You own a lawn-mower or are dreaming about having a lawn to mow
- You buy your first ever T-shirt without any writing on it
- You become powerless to resist the lure of self-assembly furniture
- You discover what a pension is all about
- You wish you had a shed
- You get a shed

I know one thing – Ezekiel ben Buzi would never forget his thirtieth birthday. We find him round about that age as we come to Ezekiel chapter 1. His birthday may have been the precipitating factor in the vision that he received. By background and training, he had been brought up to believe that when he reached thirty, he would begin his life's work. He'd been trained as a priest; that was his family background. All his life had been building up to this great moment when he'd be ordained to serve in the temple in Jerusalem. He looked on it as a great privilege. So on his thirtieth birthday, you would have forgiven Ezekiel if he woke up feeling discouraged.

A crisis of faith

First of all, the success of Babylon created a crisis of faith. The unthinkable had happened. For more than one hundred years, that kingdom of Judah had been a vassal state to the great empire of Assyria. But as Assyria's power began to decline, other powers in the region, Egypt and Babylon, struggled for predominance. Often the area they fought out their rivalry in was Judah. In the year 605, a brilliant Babylonian general named Nebuchadnezzar crushed the Egyptians at the Battle of Carchemish and began systematically to subdue all the little statelets around. He took some hostages back to Babylon, including Daniel and his three friends. A few years later, Jehoiachim the king rebelled. Nebuchadnezzar besieged Jerusalem and the king died during the siege. This time Nebuchadnezzar took back with him temple treasure, some of the nobility, some of the royal family, some priests, and a substantial group of fighting men. Among them was this trainee priest, aged twenty-five. Ten years later Zedekiah, the king installed by Nebuchadnezzar, was going to rebel, there was to be an eighteen month siege. The army would be destroyed, the city burned, the temple demolished and the population almost entirely deported. The day that Ezekiel turned thirty, he was five years into his captivity in Babylon.

Where was God?

The success of Babylon created a crisis of faith. The Jews had all the promises of God, but where was He in their circumstances? Was the God of Israel no more than a myth? Since all the rival gods of

Babylon seemed to be victorious, did that mean their God didn't have the power to resist the gods of Babylon? Had they not been led to think that the royal throne of Judah would last for ever? Now it was destroyed. Had they not been led to think of Israel as a world power, with a commonwealth that would draw in all the nations? Yet the northern kingdom had disappeared and now Judah was a vassal state. What had become of God's promises?

It wasn't just the success of Babylon, it was also the pluralism they found in Babylon that was a challenge to them. They found themselves literally in a foreign land; not just geographically but also spiritually. When they visited Babylon, they would have found religion of the liquorice allsorts variety – there were hundreds of gods, and hundreds of shrines dedicated to an assortment of other earthly and heavenly deities. Babylon must have seemed so grand compared to Jerusalem. But here was the troubling thing: no matter where you went in Babylon, you would not find one trace of the God of Judah; not one shrine, altar, or temple. What a temptation to think maybe their God didn't exist at all.

Maybe some tragedy or event has left you asking similar questions. Where is God? Why doesn't He say something? Rather than triumph, I'm experiencing defeat. Rather than victory over temptation, I'm falling to temptation over and over again. Where is God? Can you blame some of these exiles in Babylon who gave up hope altogether?

God reveals His glory

On his thirtieth birthday Ezekiel had what every one of us needs – a vision of God. First God reveals His glory to this man. The first part of Ezekiel is all about wheels within wheels and creatures with strange faces and so on, but what in fact we have in Ezekiel chapter 1 is the vision of the glory of God. God's glory is the visible manifestation of His presence. When we talk about the glory of God, what we are saying is that the invisible becomes visible, usually with a very powerful high-profile impact on those that are watching and seeing. Moses had an impactful vision of the glory of God at Mount Sinai and his face shone as a result. When Solomon first dedicated the first temple there was the glory cloud, the Shekinah, that came and filled the temple; a vision of God becoming visible before His people. That's what Ezekiel saw, verse 1, the heavens opened, the curtain was drawn and he saw behind the curtain to where God is in all His splendour and glory.

A vision is not given to us to visualise in our minds, but to interpret, with the Bible offering the key to what the signs and symbols mean. The first thing here is the mobility of God (5-21). This is not a static vision. A storm that races across the desert, the living creatures with their legs and their wings, the wheels within wheels spinning around – all of it describes a scene of motion, action, speed. The Lion of Judah is not caged back there in Jerusalem, He is restless and is marching around, with Ezekiel in Babylon in the midst of his exile. There's been a lot of discussion about the wheels within wheels (15-21). The picture painted is of a massive war chariot, with this exception – normally a chariot can only move backwards and forwards. This chariot, however, is a multi-directional chariot. If you're ever tried to parallel park your car, you'll know how difficult it is to get into a limited space, and you might have dreamed of a machine like this – like one of those office chairs that you can move any way you want to. This chariot can move not only backwards, forwards and sideways, this chariot can move up and down as well. It can move in any direction it wants to, at the speed of light or faster; it's an amazing motion-filled picture that is painted here. Verses 20 and 21 tell us why. It is because it is driven by the Spirit of God: wherever the Spirit would go, they would go.

The majesty of God

A number of things point us to this. There's the imagery of the Lord riding in a storm, surrounded by fire and lightning (4). That's a common way of describing the divine warrior; storms and clouds are often associated in the Bible with theophanies, that is, appearances of God. The ultimate theophany that we look forward to is the glory cloud and the splendour and the lightning flash when the Lord Jesus comes back in the clouds of majesty. Then there are the attendants of the glory and majesty of God, the cherubim (4-14). These cherubs are not cute. They bear no resemblance to the rosy-cheeked figures of popular mythology. They have four faces: the face of a man, the highest of all God's creation, man being generic of both male and female there; the lion, the highest wild animal; the ox, the highest domestic animal; the eagle, the highest bird. They embody within themselves all the highest attributes of living creation. The cherubim are the guardians of God's holiness, His heavenly bodyguard. They're the ones that keep Isaiah away when he's in the temple and they cry, 'Holy, holy, holy, Lord God Almighty! The whole earth is full of Your glory!'

They are also God's law enforcers. It's the cherubim at the gate of the Garden of Eden with their swords drawn, barring the way back into God's presence for those who have rebelled. They are there in this vision, which is not meant simply to comfort Ezekiel. This is not simply the quiet time to end all quiet times: there is a scary aspect to the glory of God because this God Who reigns in glory is moving to judge His own people. Judgement always begins at the house of God, so the mood of the vision is both threatening and hopeful. But as in Genesis, there is also among the dark clouds of judgement the trace of the rainbow which has always promised hope and mercy to a rebellious world. He is coming to judge but He is signalling that there is mercy that is wrapped around His judgement. In wrath He will remember mercy.

The throne of God

This is the next thing that underlines the majesty of God. The throne is the centre of the vision itself. Here Ezekiel's language virtually breaks down. He is straining at language and imagery to convey to us this vision of the splendour of the glory of God. You can't describe God. Read down these chapters: often he repeats phrases like these: 'what looked like'; 'the appearance of': in other words, what he sees looks like a throne. The figure on the throne has the appearance of a man, it is God in human form. In fact, the word for 'likeness' there is first used in Genesis 1:26, of God creating human beings in His own image. Here is God in the likeness of a man, that's the vision that he has.

One of the keys to understanding this book of Ezekiel is to know that John in Revelation draws from its imagery and metaphors. In Revelation chapter 1, John tells us that he sees someone similar to Ezekiel's vision: one like a son of man, dressed in a robe reaching down to His feet with a golden sash around His chest, His head and hair white as snow, eyes like blazing fire. He is seeing the Lord Jesus on the throne.

Don't you and I need to see the sovereign Lord in our day? In our part of the world the church is in decline, our buildings are mainly empty. Our impact on the nation is marginal at best and there are moments of clear-sighted honesty when we ask ourselves, is the cause of Christ lost in our day in our land? What we need to see more than anything else is this vision of the glory of God: the mobile, majestic God, Who is in charge not just in Zion, His holy hill – He is in charge in Babylon in exile, where we are, far from home. What the people of God in exile most needed to see was that the sovereign Lord was as much in Babylon as He was in Jerusalem. The same Lord who led them out of exile in Egypt is still Lord of His church here in western Europe today, the same mobile, majestic Lord Who is saying to us, 'The whole world is Mine, I have territorial demands and I am making them on the whole earth; the whole earth will be filled with the glory of God.'

When Ezekiel sees the glory of God, where does he go? He goes down on his face before the glory of God. That is always what happens when someone is overcome with the majesty and glory of His name. He sees a vision of the appearance of the likeness of the glory of God (verse 28) and when he saw it, he says: 'I fell face down'. The glory of God appeared once in the shape of a man, and Peter said 'Go away from me, Lord, I'm unclean.' The glory of God appeared to John on the Isle of Patmos, 'and when I saw Him' he says, 'I fell at His feet as though dead.' We need to see the glory of God in western Europe in the twenty-first century.

God shares his burden

This book shows us the connections between Ezekiel and the book of Revelation. Both books begin with a theophany – an appearance of God in Christ. Both have a similar message. In Revelation the Lord Jesus is walking among the churches; both here in Ezekiel and in Revelation, we're given the picture of God among His people wherever they are. He threatens His people – and that is no idle threat. Ezekiel hears God speak about a disobedient people. When you glance through chapter 2 you'll find a recurrence of the word rebel and rebellious; that's how God saw His people. No other people had had so much done for them as these people had, nor had so consistently rejected the word and the will of God. Chapter 2:3; like a rebellious vassal state, they had sided with the enemy instead of with their liege Lord.

In chapter 2 we discover the root of every sin. It is rebellion, a refusal to recognise God's sovereignty over us. Romans 1 says, 'What is it we do with God's truth? We put a lid on it. We don't want people to come and tell us about it. Every human being knows the truth of God and has put a lid on it in their unrighteousness. That is why we need such a great salvation.' This is a disobedient race (2:4), a hardened people.

Ezekiel's calling was not to be an easy one. He was not being sent to the Gentiles, like a Wycliffe missionary, to go into an area that has never heard the truth, that doesn't even have the word of God in its own language. If that had been the job that Ezekiel had been given, God says to him, 'That would be an easier job than the one I'm giving you. If I was sending you to some remote tribe, they would listen to the word I am giving you. But these people will not listen to what I'm saying. Though they have the Scriptures, though they know you're My servant, they're not going to listen to you.'

In these verses in the original Hebrew, the word *goyim*, which is usually used of the Gentile nations, is applied to the Jewish people, the people of God. The chosen nation has become the unchosen nation, for they will not only not listen to Ezekiel, they will not listen to God through Ezekiel. Chris Wright in his commentary points out this, 'it is still tragically true that in some parts of the world the challenge of God's word receives a better hearing among those who have never heard it than among those established churches who have grown hard and deaf in their resistance to the movements of God's Spirit'. Remember Jesus when he spoke in Revelation: 'Let those who have an ear to hear, hear what the Spirit is saying to the churches.' To be a servant in these days means sharing God's heart, His burden for His people and the world in its hardened and disobedient state.

God issues his call

Ezekiel is not on his knees very long before the Spirit comes (2:1) and tells him to stand up; prostration must give way to action. God comes to him entirely unsought and reveals Himself to him, to commission him for a task and to entrust him with a message. If God speaks to you from His word, He is speaking to you so He might push you into His service. The call of God to Ezekiel is to swim against the popular tide. It's a call to take God's word seriously, to live a life of compliant obedience to that word: specifically, to do two things. First he is called to be a spokesman (2:7). 'You must listen,' verse 8, 'to what I say to you.' That's compliant obedience to God.

Like all prophets, this prophet was not going to enjoy the luxury of deciding which message to deliver, or which audience to go to. Nor would he be able to make his response conditional on how they reacted to him. In an age such as ours, driven by the need to have a successful ministry, usually defined as larger and larger congregations, we need to learn that God's call sometimes is to the tough job of simply being His spokesman in an unpopular age.

In order to be God's spokesman, what is he to do (3:1)? He is to eat what is before him, to consume and then to proclaim the word of God. He is to absorb the word of God into the totality of his life. And that will be a bittersweet experience. On the one hand there is the sweetness of the word of God that thrills the heart, that energises the whole being, so you want somebody to listen to what you have to say. But it's a bittersweet experience because not everybody out there is waiting for you to tell them what God has to say, the truths that have burst into your mind and heart. You may be rejected for what you have to say. You may find that when you're trying to bring the conversation round to spiritual truths, their minds are far away.

Ezekiel is unique, a prophet of God. But we live in a different age from Ezekiel, the age of the Spirit, where He has been poured out on all God's people. We live in the age of the prophet-hood of all believers. We are all called to be witnesses about Jesus Christ. We have been given a book that we are to take and inwardly digest. We have not been handed a blank sheet on which we can write our own message for the twenty-first century, but a book that is written on both sides, so there's no room for addition. We are to take it in its entirety into our hearts and lives, and then proclaim it to men and women. We stand alongside Ezekiel, with a common task of being God's spokesmen in a world that needs to hear what God is saying.

The watchman

Secondly, he was called to be a watchman. What's the key idea behind this? It's the idea of responsibility. What's the job of the watchman? It's to cry 'Danger!' When we were small boys, we used to go and play in someone else's back yard. It was often my job to keep an eye out for the owner. I was the watchman. And I'm still a watchman. Every preacher of the gospel is a watchman. Every Christian who lives in an alien society where the people around them are going to hell, to a Christless eternity, they're watchmen. What was Ezekiel's job? It was to cry 'Danger!' There's judgement coming, the wrath of God is revealed from heaven against all the ungodliness and unrighteousness of men. I dare not be silent about judgement, to pretend that that bit isn't in the Bible, or that bit does not belong to the good news message of the gospel. I dare not listen to Jesus as He comes along in His preaching ministry, warning of judgement and then ignore it. We are called to be watchmen in our day and generation, every bit as much as Ezekiel was in his day and generation. There is an enemy out there.

Of course there were other preachers in Ezekiel's day, as there were in Jeremiah's day, and they fudged the message of judgement. Jeremiah tells us about these people: 'From the least of them to the greatest, they all alike practise deceit. They dress the wound of my people as though it were not serious. "Peace, peace" they say, when there is no peace.' From how many pulpits in this country are there those who are saying to those who are lost and undone, 'peace, peace', when there is no peace? Ezekiel is given this great task of saying 'There is judgement coming. Flee from the wrath to come.' The wrath of the Lamb is the fiercest of all wraths. And we are accountable. 'I will hold you accountable,' He says, 'for their blood.'

Aren't we God's spokesmen and God's watchmen to our generation? Don't we have to say to people, as Rico Tice put it in *Christianity Explored*, that we are more wicked than we ever imagined and more loved than we dared believe? We need to tell people the bad news as well as the good news.

God equips his servant

For great as God is – and we are meant, by the way, to see the great contrast in these verses between God, who is described again and again as the sovereign Lord, and the description God uses of Ezekiel, 'son of man'. It emphasises Ezekiel's humanity and mortality, opposed to God who is the sovereign Lord. How is God going to do His work in the world? He is going to do His work in the world through a son of man, a human vehicle. He wants this human vehicle to know that this job he's got is going to be a tough job. He doesn't want him to feel cheated.

Why is the vision being given? First, because God wanted to encourage him with His presence. He wanted Ezekiel to know that he was the God of the whole earth and was going to be with him wherever he was. Jesus said, 'I am with you always' – when you go into the office, or the factory, you're sitting beside your friend at school or university, you're sitting beside your neighbour and you're there as Jesus' witness – God is present with you.

Second, God's Spirit strengthened this man. Central to this vision is the Spirit of God (2:2). I imagine Ezekiel might have preferred to lie there on the ground, awed by the majesty of God. But it isn't paralysis that God wants, it is reasonable service. God raises him by the Spirit to his feet. It is the Spirit who strengthens Ezekiel (3:8,9). It is the Spirit who makes him as tough as his opponents, and (3:12) it's the Spirit who sets him on his feet, deposits him among the exiles, puts him in the place of service, and equips him for the task.

Wherever God calls us, He equips us for the ministry to which He has called us, and He is going to accomplish His work in the world through a son of man. That is actually one of the great themes of Ezekiel. God is going to accomplish his work through this man, because He's called this man to be absolutely obedient to His word. He's going to accomplish His work among the exiles through a son of man who obeys His word and Who is committed to suffer whatever God sends along His path in order to accomplish the will of God. Have you heard that anywhere else in the Bible? I think that's at least one of the reasons Jesus prefers the title, 'Son of Man' in the Gospels. Not just the vision of the heavenly being of Daniel's vision but also the son of man image in Ezekiel, the son of man Who suffers, serves and speaks the word of God. God is going to accomplish His purpose ultimately through the Son of Man who would come into the world.

Let's summarise where we've come so far. Ezekiel challenges our vision of God. What are you thinking about God? How has your mind changed about God? Do you think that He is limited to times in the past? I've just become minister of a church where God did mighty things back in the 1940s and 1950s, following Alan Redpath and Stephen Olford and hearing the great stories of how they filled the great theatre next door. The great temptation would be to think that that's when God was working. Fortunately we have some real great prayer warriors who were very active in those days and they believe God can do it again. Maybe you think God's tied to the past – Wesley, Whitefield, or back to Luther and Calvin, or right back to the first century. You think it was all right for God then, but not today. Or maybe you limit God geographically. God works in church on Sunday, when we're altogether worshipping, but not where I am, in the current thrust of my everyday life. You need a vision of a God who is mobile and majestic, the sovereign protector. It challenges our motivation. What was to motivate Ezekiel? He was to bring glory to God through faithful obedience. He was to listen and speak the word that God had given to him. We are called to do exactly the same in our generation.

Thirdly, it's a challenge to our dependence. It's interesting that Ezekiel couldn't even stand up without the Spirit lifting him, in chapter 2:1. Yet we seem able to stand up, preach, plan, counsel and minister without the Spirit. We seem happy to sit in our studies and prepare our talks, to go to church, plan our programmes and run our ministries. Occasionally we bemoan the fact that we don't pray any more, we don't have prayer meetings any more, people won't come to prayer meetings any more – but we get on with the job! Ezekiel couldn't do anything without the Spirit strengthening him. We seem to follow a practical theology of self-reliance whereas God wants to teach us how to wait patiently on Him. Are you feeling disturbed by the fact that the world seems to have won? Then you need to come back and look at this vision of this almighty mobile majestic God, until you're able to say with the apostle Paul, 'I am convinced that neither death nor life, neither angels nor demons, neither the present nor the future, nor any powers, neither height nor depth nor anything else in all creation, will be able to separate us from the love of God that is in Christ Jesus, our Lord.' Amen.

When God leaves the building
Chapters 8 – 11

Introduction

Dad came home from work one night and his teenage son came into the living room and said, 'Dad I've got some bad news and some good news for you.' Dad, who was exhausted after a busy day, said, 'I can't cope with the bad news right now. Tell me the good news first.' 'The good news is,' said the boy, 'the air bag in your BMW works perfectly.'

The book of Ezekiel is a bad news/good news book. The first section tells of the coming devastation of Jerusalem. In a whole variety of ways, Ezekiel is given this charge of communicating how serious God is in bringing judgement upon Jerusalem. The people don't want to believe it. The great challenge that he faces in the first part of the book is of getting secured in their minds the fact that God has made threats as well as given promises and that God is serious in both.

It's only after he's laid this foundation and told them precisely what is going to happen in Jerusalem that he earns their respect and the credibility required for them to listen when he speaks in part two of the good news of even greater things in the future. They've seen God do exactly what he predicts, so they're much more willing to listen to him as he speaks of this wonderful future that God is preparing.

One of the reasons why the people of his day did not believe that Judah and Jerusalem were going to be devastated was because they believed that God would never abandon Jerusalem, because of the temple. Jeremiah had mocked the people for their false confidence in the temple. They repeated (Jer. 7:4) 'The temple of the LORD!' as if simply repeating those words meant that they were protected supernaturally from danger. Ezekiel is about to shatter those illusions. This section is the darkest. It describes the corrupted worship of God. This is no debate about styles of worship, ancient and modern: this is to do with false and true worship, the behaviour of God's people which has provoked God to jealousy.

The acts of Ezekiel (8:1-4)

Fourteen months have passed since we saw him yesterday, receiving his call from God on his thirtieth birthday. In the intervening time, Ezekiel has been bizarrely busy. He has been performing a series of sign acts to get the people's attention. First, he drew an outline of the cityscape of Jerusalem. They would have immediately recognised it. After he'd drawn that, he built himself a little diorama, a kind of miniature city, with soldiers circling it like a city under siege. That was fine: the people recognised here was a city besieged, a picture of Jerusalem.

Then he lay down on the ground, at the same time every day, in a kind of east-west direction with his back to the picture of Jerusalem, facing the city that was besieged, on the ground, and he got himself an iron pan. He put it between his face and the city and he growled at it. He did that every day. Every day the people would walk past and look at Ezekiel. Day 32, day 54, he's still doing the same thing. Suddenly it twigs in their heads: he's facing north, his back's towards Jerusalem, he's visualising what happened one hundred years back, to Samaria, the northern kingdom. It had disappeared altogether: they were sunk in all kinds of idolatry and God had obliterated the northern ten tribes of Israel. As they looked at this, they thought, 'That's right. God was angry with Israel.' Day 200, day 324, day 374, they're getting the message. 'God was angry with those people because of their idolatry, they deserved to be devastated, obliterated,' they're all saying. 'Amen, preach it, brother!'

They're getting used to this. Day 391: he moves the cityscape down a bit, he moves the little diorama down towards his drawing of Jerusalem, puts it down there, lies down – this time he's not facing north, he's facing south – gets his pan and growls at it. They were getting the message: the God who had acted against the northern kingdom of Israel is going to act against the southern kingdom of Judah and Jerusalem. God is angry; the wrath of God is being revealed against His people because of their sin. Ezekiel regularly has to argue for the righteousness of God in the way in which He deals with His people, and we find that happening here in chapters 8 to 11. There would have been those, then as now, who would be uncomfortable with God being angry with His people.

One day, some of the leaders of the people came to Ezekiel, hoping that he would tell them the city would be all right; God would rescue them. As they're sitting round, suddenly Ezekiel is caught up into a vision. He sees the appearance of a man, one he had seen earlier, that pre-incarnate appearance of the Lord Jesus. He seems to be travelling somewhere. They could see the physical reactions as he is taken by high-speed travel from where he is (in his mind, that is, in this vision) back to Jerusalem. He is lifted by the hair and pulled from where he is in Babylon to Jerusalem. Then he is given this virtual reality tour of the temple. God is showing him why He is angry with His people, and what he sees is both shocking and frightening.

Provocation! (8:5-18)

What has provoked God to jealousy? God is giving him a view of the temple, starting on the outside and then taking him progressively closer into the very heart of the temple precincts, right to the place where the Holy of Holies and God's presence was. He's met by the glory of God and we discover God is provoked to jealousy by false worship.

False worship

The first scene from verse 5 onwards takes place outside the temple, on the main route over which the public would walk. Straddling this main route is the goddess Asherah, a Canaanite mother goddess, thought of in the ancient world as being the consort of the God of Israel. The worship of the goddess Asherah involved all kinds of sexual immorality and God says, 'This provokes me to jealousy.' The word used is of a betrayed lover. Here is the way God feels when His redeemed people break His covenant: God is saying wherever His people turn towards some other source of help, some other god, He will not hang around any longer. He will simply be off, for the God of Israel is a sensitive God, every bit as much as the Holy Spirit is a sensitive Spirit who can be grieved, resisted or provoked to jealousy.

The glory takes Ezekiel further in, to this scene where there are seventy elders, the lay figures of Judah. They're meeting in little rooms off the main sanctuary and the walls are covered with all kinds of creatures. These are demonic forces worshipped by the Egyptians. The elders were business leaders, key people in the community, who had their own private club on the temple precincts. They may have thought 'The Egyptians might win this great power struggle between Egypt and Babylon; we may want to be in with them. Why don't we get ready by worshipping their powerful gods?' It's like a person who joins a secret society or club to advance their business interests and compromises their Christian testimony. They were saying to one another, God doesn't see us, He's deserted us, so we need other sources of help. The essence of idolatry is not so much that we deny the reality of God, but that we deny the relevance of God in our circumstances, and we look elsewhere for help and encouragement.

The third scene (verses 14,15), is a group of women weeping for Tammuz, a Babylonian deity, at the north gate of the temple itself. This was a god of nature with a particular appeal to women. The fourth scene is even more frightening still. From verse 16 onwards, Ezekiel is taken right into the very heart of the temple, next to the altar itself, reserved for the priests and the Levites, immediately in front of the Holy of Holies. In that sacred spot outside the great curtain of the Holy of Holies, these people are bowing down with their bottoms up to the Holy of Holies and their heads down to the rising sun coming from the east, quite deliberately. Later on it says they were giving the middle finger to God, that is how bad the word is in the original. It is a terrible picture of people who are disregarding God. They're changing the truth of God into a lie, worshipping Shamash the Babylonian sun god, and they're effectively saying, 'Babylon is going to win.'

Fudged worship

God is provoked to jealousy by false worship and by fudged worship. The real point of chapter 8 is that all of this is going on in the very temple where God is being worshipped. These people hadn't stopped worshipping the God of Israel: they were just not sure that they could get by with His help alone, so they're covering themselves spiritually and politically. Rather than just trusting God, they're putting themselves in a position where they could get help from other sources. This is the ultimate multi-faith service – and here is God's view of it. God hates fudged worship. God is provoked to jealousy by it.

We must get out of our minds the limited idea of worship that we have – as the singing or the meeting. Worship is the whole response of our lives towards God as God has revealed Himself. Those last words are crucial. The only God there is to worship is the God Who has revealed Himself to us in the Bible in Jesus Christ. No other god is God at all. No matter how much the teaching of that god may approximate to some aspects of Christian teaching, the only God there is, is the God and Father of our Lord Jesus Christ. That is how He has revealed Himself to us, and anyone worshipping a god by any other name is worshipping an idol. It matters intensely to God, what we believe about Him.

These people were not prepared to accept God's verdict on their nation. They were trying to find political solutions to spiritual problems and God finds it an abomination. They were prepared to worship God so long as their worship is modified by the new realities of life in their world, in which the gods of Babylon are obviously strong. We are living in a New Age world that would say to you, 'We need to acknowledge these other forces, the forces of nature, the Celtic superstitions – we need to recognise these things, we need to bring them all together and acknowledge them.'

What does God feel about that? Read Ezekiel 8 and you cannot escape this conclusion: God hates that. He is provoked to jealousy. God makes no comment on the people of the Canaanites worshipping their Canaanite god or the people of Babylon worshipping their Babylonian deities. He is provoked to jealousy when His people, who believe that He is the God Who has acted in the past, when they prostitute themselves to other idols. When His own people want to maintain their private faith in Him but want to say that the anti-God ideas, accepted by society around us, have won the day, those people provoke Him to jealousy.

Romans 12:2 says, 'Don't let the world around you squeeze you into its mould.' Are we letting that happen? Do we shy away from God talk because it's unfashionable? Do we prefer to focus on felt needs rather than on the transcendent God? Have we privatised our religion and our values, content to share our feelings about different issues but unwilling to acknowledge that we know where absolute truth lies? Do we want to justify Christianity not on the grounds that it is true, but on the pragmatic grounds that it simply is one of the best, or better self-improvement programmes? Do we trivialise our faith to make it more acceptable to a generation fixated on television? Is the God that we proclaim just another therapist whose greatest joy is to help people feel good about themselves? These too are idolatries and they make God jealous for His glory among His people. We are to be very tolerant of those outside of Christ who may be buried in idolatry of one kind or another. The lesson of chapter 8 is that we must be intolerant of idolatry among ourselves. He will not be treated simply as one option among many. 'I am the Lord your God, you shall have no other gods before Me.'

Vindication! (9:1-11)

Up to now the glory of God has been an onlooker at these activities but in chapter 9 we find the intervention of the Lord (4-7). There is a terrible description of slaughter (5-6). This a vision, not something that he is seeing happening before his eyes, but in the vision the slaughter is the natural and just consequence of the sin he has just described. God is not indifferent to human sin. He does not shut his eyes to our rebellion against Him. He is slow to act. The vision begins with the glory of God watching these activities. He has not acted while all these idolatrous practices were taking place. For centuries the glory of God has been inactive as one king after another in Israel and Judah had come along and led the people into one idolatrous action after another. God had been patient. But now the patience has come to an end.

God is going to move. Judgement cannot be held back for ever and notice where it begins (9:6). Where do you think God begins when He looks at the world? Do you think God begins with non-Christian religions? 1 Peter 4:17 says, 'Judgement must begin at the house of the Lord, for if the righteous scarcely be saved, where do the unrighteous and Godless appear?' Where does God begin when He comes to investigate the world today? He begins with us, with the believer whose body is a temple of the Holy Spirit. 'Do you not know that your body is a temple of the Holy Spirit, Who is in you, Whom you have received from God? You are not your own; you were bought at a price. Therefore honour God with your body' (1 Cor. 6:19,20). What are we doing in the body? Are we prostituting it before the idol of sex? Are we pampering it in self-indulgence? Are we abusing it in some way or other?

What do you think the Lord thinks about the Christian who professes to believe in the sovereignty of God on Sunday and yet in the practicalities of his everyday life resorts to finding worldly solutions to problems? Or who as well as following Jesus, reads their stars and tries to see a compatibility between astrology and the occult, and their Christian faith? What does He think about the believer who swears allegiance to the Lordship of Christ on Sunday but serves the bottom line for the rest of the week?

God visits His church

Where does God go next? He goes to His church, His covenant people; they too corporately are His temple. Whoever would destroy

God's church would destroy God's temple. What does He think of our churches? What does He make of our self-indulgent preoccupation with our internal politics when there is a world outside lost and going to hell? What does He think about our half-heartedness in evangelism, our toying with New Age ideas, our tolerance of old heresies, our questioning of some of the basic truths of the Bible, our elevation of subjective experience over the objective truth of what is in the Bible? What does He think about our ordaining those who are prepared to question or deny the resurrection of the Lord Jesus? What does He think about a church that, in the interests of appearing relevant to popular culture, is prepared to ditch or play down the more embarrassing aspects of Christian belief? How does He react to those who think they can proclaim Jesus and not mention judgement? Do you think He's indifferent to these things? Do you think He will tolerate this for ever? Remember the dire warnings of Jesus to the churches of Asia Minor: repent or your candlestick will be removed.

Jerusalem, the holy city, was to fall twice. Once within a few years of Ezekiel speaking these words and once again in AD70. For in spite of all the warnings, the prophets, the words of God and the arrival of God Himself in the temple, they rejected Him, and God removed the candlestick of witness. Where are the seven churches of Revelation? They didn't have the ears to hear what the Spirit says to the churches. They vanished. God is provoked to jealousy. Some of the great preaching centres in our own land today are furniture warehouses or trendy apartments. What Christ does expect is that His people will not play the game of a Godless society. He expects that His people will resist the world's pull, living counter-cultural lives, questioning the world's values and living by Jesus' commands, even when that is unpopular.

Judgement in action

Notice the angel is commanded to go through the city (3-6), putting a mark on the foreheads of those who grieve and lament over all the detestable things that are done. Even God's true believing people are caught up as collateral damage whenever the judgement falls. Many true believers were going to die when the city was eventually sacked and destroyed. Revelation 7:3 talks about the mark, the seal of God on the foreheads of the servants of the Lord. These were not necessarily influential people: all we're told is that they had the mark of grace on them. They grieved over all the detestable things that were done in the city. They had a broken and contrite spirit, they wept over the sin of their church and their nation. They repudiated the standards of the people around them; they were being renewed in the spirit of their minds. Like Daniel, they were coming to God and there was no spirit of criticism in them. They were not saying, 'Do something about them.' They were saying, 'Forgive me for my sin.'

They have the mark of God upon them. The word 'mark' there in the Hebrew is the last letter in the Hebrew alphabet which is written in the form of a slanting cross. In Revelation the names of the Father and of the Lamb are written on the foreheads of the faithful. It reminds us of that protective mark, the dab of blood from the Passover lamb put on the doors of Hebrew homes as the angel of death comes to visit. In the Greek script, the sign of the slanting cross is the first letter of the name of Christ, and in the Bible's larger storyline, the mercy of God in the midst of judgement finds its ultimate expression in the Person of Jesus, the Christ. He is the One Who saves us from the coming wrath.

Chapter 9:7-8 tells of the intercession of the prophet. He cries out, 'Sovereign LORD, are you going to destroy the entire remnant?' because he is moved with compassion for those who are under judgement. The picture of hell was not given to us for academic debate, it was to warn us of real danger and to push us into genuine intercession for the world. Maybe the reason we don't pray any more is we don't believe people are going to hell any more.

Relocation!

Chapter 11 opens with a small group of conspirators plotting together. They saw property prices falling and were saying, 'This can't go on for ever. The Egyptians will deliver us, and then property prices will start going up again. Now is the time for us to buy up all the property.' There were also denying the final collapse of the city; they believed it would never fall into the hands of the Babylonians. God would not let it happen. They were saying to one another (11:3), 'It is not near.'

There are still people today who believe that everything can be fixed by money, technology or military might, but I remember when communism collapsed with frightening rapidity. What would it take to bring collapse to western civilisation? A few commercial and industrial exposures of fraud, that brings a total loss of confidence to world markets, a collapse to world trade? Some major terrorist incidents? A breakdown in law and order? There is no God-given right for western civilisation to last any longer than Roman civilisation did. Don't put your confidence in the west, or in democracy. Put your confidence in the living God Who will do as He pleases in His world.

The glory is departing

Jerusalem is deserted. Shocking though that may be, unbelievable to the average believing Jew in that age, it falls. God is moving somewhere else (9:3). The winged chariot begin to move (10:4,5); the glory of the Lord departs from the threshold of the temple (18). Then in chapter 11 verses 22 to 24, the glory of the Lord went up out of the city and stopped above the mountain.

The God of the Bible is not a God of any place but the God of people. He is a God Who is passionately concerned for the spiritual life of His people. He is prepared to sacrifice their reputation, comfort, and success, if He can bring them back to that place where they are purified, repentant and effective for Him again. He is far more concerned for the holiness of His people than He is for their happiness. John Calvin comments, 'The scourges of God are more useful to us because when God indulges us we abuse his clemency and flatter ourselves and grow hardened in our sin.' We Christian people don't do well in good days. We grow fat, flabby and lazy and need preaching that challenges the popular idolatries of our day. Listen to these words by Richard Lovelace

We may need to challenge more and comfort less in our evangelism and discipleship. We need to make it harder for people to retain assurance of salvation when they move into serious sin. We need to tell some people who think they have gotten saved to get lost. The puritans were biblically realistic about this. We have become sloppy and sentimental in promoting assurance under any circumstances.

It's a very dark picture but it isn't all dark. At the end of chapter 11, we find positive words of hope. What is God's goal in all this? Verse 20: 'They will be My people and I will be their God.'

Idolatry

How do you measure your success in life? This is often a way for us to assess the extent to which idolatry has moved into our hearts. If we sacrifice relationships to win the blessing of the god 'career', we're idolaters. If we squander the precious hours of our lives for the god 'entertainment', we are idolaters. If we crave the self-affirmation we get from sex or power, we are idolaters. If our self-worth is measured by our net worth, we are idolaters. If we are ashamed to assert our belief in an infinite Creator God for fear of being treated as intellectual pygmies by the world outside, we are idolaters. We've allowed a secular idolatry to dominate our minds. Listen to these words by C.S. Lewis

> If we consider the unblushing promises of reward and the staggering nature of the rewards promised us in the Gospels, it would seem that the Lord finds our desires not too strong but too weak. We are half-hearted creatures, fooling around with drink and sex and ambition when infinite joy is offered us. Like an ignorant child who wants to go on making mud pies in a slum because he cannot understand what is meant by the offer of a holiday by the seaside, we are far too easily pleased.

The glory departs from Jerusalem, just as the glory has departed from many churches in the western world. Notice where the glory goes when it departs. It hovers above a mountain (11:23) to the east of Jerusalem, the Mount of Olives. Five hundred years later, the glory of God was going to be visiting the temple again, this time not as a cloud of fire, not with cherubim, but in a person: 'We beheld His glory, the glory of the One and Only God'. The glory of God revisited the temple. He came twice and on both occasions, He clears the temple. He is looking for righteousness and finds unrighteousness. He is looking for holiness and finds unholiness, for true worship and finding a den of thieves. The glory comes and the glory leaves, pausing at the city gate to be crucified, stripped, scorned and ill-treated. The glory leaves and pauses again on the Mount of Olives, to give His last words to His church to go into all the world. His people were to claim the whole world for His kingship. People from every tribe and tongue and nation were to be gathered under the kingship of this one King who comes in the name of the Lord.

On that mountain He promised to be with His people wherever they went, to the ends of the age. That presence can be found wherever His people are, even when they find themselves exiled in a strange land. And to that Mount of Olives He will come again, in power and glory. When the kingdoms of this world become the kingdoms of our God and of His Christ, and He reigns for ever and ever and every creature, the cherubim and the redeemed will gather together their voices and sing, 'Hallelujah! For the Lord God, the Almighty, reigns!' Amen.

The Good Shepherd
Chapter 34

Introduction

In Ezekiel from chapters 8 to 10 to chapter 33, there's a lot of recapitulation. The themes of idolatry and the coming destruction of Jerusalem, the idea that God would ever use a foreign nation like Babylon, or any other foreign nation, as His servant to do His bidding under His sovereign rule, all are explored and expanded. One of the themes that is emphasised is the tendency among the people of God to blame previous generations for the mess they found themselves in. They kept quoting (18:2) a proverb that was popular, 'The fathers eat sour grapes and the children's teeth are set on edge.' What they were saying was 'Whatever is happening to us, however we are behaving now isn't our fault, we're not to blame. It's a generational sin. We're making the choices we're making because of the influences of previous generations.'

Ezekiel is quite clear. He repeats a phrase over and over in that chapter: 'The soul who sins is the one who will die.' There is a big difference between saying that the consequences of a previous generation's sins can be handed on to succeeding generations – it is another thing to say that I make the choices that I make because of what someone did in the past. 'The soul that sins, it shall die' – those people were responsible for their own sins. He's emphasised that but saying that everybody is responsible for their own sin does not mean that there aren't some people who are more responsible than others for the state of God's people in that age. That's the theme that he's now picking up in chapter 34 as he introduces us to the great promise of the future in the purpose of God.

Here is this man, a faithful spokesman, passing on what God has told him to say, a faithful watchman who has cried out fearlessly about the dangers that are ahead. All the other false prophets are saying to the people, 'peace, peace' when there is no peace. Ezekiel is saying, 'The city will be destroyed, judgement will fall.' God reassures him at the end of chapter 33: when all this comes true, then they will know that a prophet has been among them. One of the helpful things for us to know as we read Ezekiel is that those first thirty-three chapters are establishing the credibility of this prophet. We can listen to Ezekiel because he has already proved his credibility.

The record of failed leadership

The issue that he raises in chapter 34 is leadership. The world is divided into three parts: there are those who make things happen, those who watch what's happening, and those who have no idea what's happening. The people who make things happen in the world are the leaders; the ones who dream dreams, who are out in front taking the risks.

Now leaders who have lost the plot are a menace. We see that nationally and in our churches. They bring frustration at best and downright misery at worst. Often a good man or woman is corrupted by high office: it happens in dictatorships and in democracies; when a leader becomes more interested in winning the next election, or having a good entry about themselves in the history book, or ensuring a nest egg for their retirement; the seeds of corruption already are being sown in their heart. Jim Graham from Gold Hill quoted this 'There are few people God can trust with power.' It's so true.

The first hopeful sign in this book is the promise of a new leader who would reign in compassion and strength and would lead the people of God into a period of unparalleled prosperity and security (23,24). Verses 1 to 16 begin by inveigling against the shepherds of Israel. The title 'shepherd' was a very familiar one in the ancient world, as a metaphor for the king or the god of a little state or country. Very often the earthly king was a representative of the divine king who had appointed him and the earthly king was seen as a kind of under-shepherd, under the leadership of the great shepherd or the god. Outside of Israel, the king could be a god himself, as in Egypt. In other religions outside of Israel the king could become the chief ruler, the chief priest, the chief prophet, but this phrase 'the shepherd' was always used to emphasise the responsibility of those in leadership to enforce social righteousness. That idea, which was common in the Middle East, was obviously also held in Israel. For example, when all the tribes came up to Hebron to make David king over them, the basis of their action (2 Sam. 5:2) was the Lord's declaration about David. Later on in Psalm 110, we find that the Messiah is going to be a shepherd who will reunite the people and rule over them as their king.

The failures of the kings

Why is God angry with the kings of Israel? Verse 6 tell us. 'They (the people) are,' He says, 'my sheep'. Those words are repeated five times in these verses. The shepherds did not own the flock, they were only employed to look after them as stewards, answerable to the Chief Shepherd. That was true of Israel under the kings; it's true of churches under their pastors and leaders. It's true in the larger sense of this world under its presidents, prime ministers or kings. Israel was God's nation. The church is God's church. The world and the nations in it are God's world, God's nations. Whoever is the leader in any of those spheres is answerable to Him. In Ezekiel's message, the Lord is coming against His shepherds, the former kings of Judah, because they've failed to fulfil their role as shepherds properly.

The monarchy of Israel had been responsible for so much of the nation's spiritual apostasy. It was the kings of Judah and Israel that had introduced idolatry into the land. It was the kings who established foreign alliances, putting their confidence in foreign powers to do for them what they'd always believed that God would do for them, protect them and ensure their security. It was the kings that enforced harsh rule which immediately threatened the reputation of the God of Israel Who was known as the compassionate and merciful God. Listen to Rehoboam as he says this: 'My father made your yoke heavy, I will make it even heavier. My father scourged you with whips; I will scourge you with scorpions.' So in chapter 34 of Ezekiel, verse 4, God complains that they have ruled the people harshly and brutally. The expression 'to rule brutally' is found in only two other places in the Old Testament. It's used of the Egyptian taskmasters who treated the Jews brutally in their bondage in Egypt, and it's used in Leviticus chapter 1 where it is forbidden to treat a fellow Israelite in this brutal manner. Even David was the one to initiate the hated system of forced labour (2 Sam. 20, 1 Kgs. 12). During Solomon's reign there was an urgent cry among the people against the level of taxation and forced labour that was going on.

So, because of the shepherds' sinful self-interest, judgement is coming on them (7-10). Because of the absence of a true shepherd; the flock, the people of God, has been scattered. God holds the kings responsible for the fact that the twelve tribes of Israel were torn apart, ten to the north and two left in the south, and made to hate each other and live in constant warfare. Ezekiel warns these false shepherds they now have an enemy greater than any they'd ever fought (10): the Lord Himself is against them.

It's a familiar picture. In many parts of the world today there are people struggling in regimes where the leadership is corrupt and where leaders are fleecing the people instead of feeding them. Such leaders need to know that one day the nations themselves will be judged. I think it applies to multi-national corporations. It applies to the scandals we're seeing where people's pensions are being destroyed because of the greed of people in leadership. God holds leaders especially accountable.

There are churches where leadership is a status symbol, a means to power for people who very often would be inadequate if they were working anywhere else. They use their facility with language or their ability to impose a guilt trip on other people in order to make them feel good about themselves. That is the nature of failed leadership.

The character of true leadership

The prophet is giving us here, among other things, a profile of what a true leader looks like and he describes it as a shepherd. Sometimes the image of a shepherd is a sentimental image. Actually a shepherd in the ancient world was regarded more as a cowboy, on the edge: a tough character, tender with his sheep, tough in the way he had to live. That's the way in which it's used here. The tough but tender shepherd can be trusted to gather, not scatter, the flock of God.

Israel had been torn in two by this internal power struggle of people who wanted to be leaders at the expense of the people of God themselves. It made God angry that people should fight for power and glory and not realise that leadership involves responsibility for the people of God, to care for them individually. This whole chapter rings with the love of God for His people. His anger with these false shepherds is motivated by His love for His sheep. There's always a danger in any form of leadership of treating people as if they are there for our convenience. A man in the ministry can be concerned merely to use people as the means for building a personal empire or outstanding reputation. And in the local church, where leaders use their skills to create division, God is angry. I'm not sure that He's very impressed with the image of the senior pastor as the chief executive officer, more concerned with budgets and bottom lines than with the people for whom Christ died. And if those principles can be applied to the leaders of churches and groups of churches, they can be applied to the leaders of small groups and ministry teams within churches – and in the secular world.

Maybe you've got people working for you. How do you treat them? Do you treat them as a shepherd looking after his sheep? Do you value your employees? Do you care for their material, spiritual and emotional needs? God holds leaders – in whatever walk of life they are – accountable for the way that they lead.

The tough and tender shepherd

The promise here is of a tough, tender shepherd who will come along and gather the scattered nation. 'I will go out and I will gather those who are lost,' says the Lord. You're going to hear that again on the lips of the Lord Jesus, Who says: 'I've come to seek and save that which was lost' (Lk. 19:10). Isaiah gives us this description of the shepherd: 'He gathers the lambs in his arms and carries them close to his heart. He gently leads those that have young.' The true leader can be trusted not to scatter but to gather the flock of God; to teach, not deceive the flock. When we use the word 'leadership', what image comes to mind? It's very hard to define in a single word but I suggest it might be 'influence'. President Harry Truman often referred to leaders as 'people who can get others to do what they don't want to do, and make them like doing it.' But get them to do what?

We need to bear in mind the background. The kings of Israel and Judah had deceived the people with bad counsel and with bad wisdom. They had counselled foreign alliances. 'All this talk about trusting the Lord, it's a bit spiritual. Don't you realise, we're living in a world where there are real armies out there with real chariots and there are enemies around. We need to make alliances with some of these other nations around us so that when we're attacked by some big power, we've got others who'll come to our aid. You can't just trust the Lord, you know.'

It was the kings who introduced foreign gods. 'Maybe, if we worship God – of course, we're not going to stop worshipping the Lord – but just to make sure that we're covering all our bases here, we're going to also just offer a little offering to this god from that country, just to appease him in case he gets angry with us. We still think our God's the chief one, of course, but we'll recognise that god over here and that god over there.'

What started with foreign alliances and foreign gods degenerated into injustice and social collapse. They served themselves, built their palaces, ate the best of food, overtaxed the people, burdened them with the heavy yoke of slavery; and so when God makes His promise about the coming shepherd He says this, 'This coming shepherd will feed the flock, He will not fleece the flock. I will place over them one shepherd.'

The shepherd in the New Testament

This idea of the shepherd feeding and tending the flock is taken up in the New Testament, and used of leadership within local churches. When Paul is speaking to the Ephesian elders in Acts 20, describing their role, he says, 'What I want you to do is to shepherd the flock of God, over which God has placed you as overseers.' If you read Acts 20, you'll discover that meant testifying to the gospel of God's grace and warning people day and night, with tears; proclaiming the whole counsel of God, not holding any bits back. That's how you tend the flock of God over which God has made you an overseer: you feed them! You don't just throw out some nice, bright ideas of how to live a good moral life. You tell them the tough news of the word of God; of judgement that's coming, of the love of God that can rescue from judgement. You proclaim the good news message of Jesus Christ and you ask the really tough questions. How does that challenge the church of Jesus Christ to live up to the gospel? Those of you who have a responsibility in local churches, whatever level it's at, you are shepherds of God's flock. Peter warns leaders to fulfil their call willingly, 'not because you must, but because you are willing, as God wants you to be; not greedy for money, but eager to serve; not lording it over those entrusted to you, but being examples to the flock' (1 Pet. 5:2,3). Make sure you're in it for the right motives. Make sure you're doing it to serve the people, be available to them. It's them you've come to care for, love, woo and win. Don't let anything get in between you and the people; love them, love them to death, love them into the kingdom, that's the role of the shepherd.

The promise of perfect leadership

The leaders of Israel and Judah had failed, and they needed a new kind of leadership. But any old leader would not do. Not even a good human leader can ultimately save or secure the flock of God. It's far too easy for a good shepherd to be struck and the sheep to be scattered. There had been good kings, who had attempted reforms in the nation. Some of them had only been half-baked reforms, others had been successful, up to a point. But even the best of these reforms had been flawed and their efforts were usually reversed by the next incumbent. So the prophet points us into the further future. He says there will be a new ruler. For the change that is to take place in Judah's situation is not so much a change in the nature of the office as in the nature of the occupant. God's solution to a history of bad shepherds is not to replace shepherding with a different system, but to replace the bad shepherds with a good shepherd.

What does he say about this shepherd? He says this good shepherd will be like David, a king after God's own heart.

The Good Shepherd

Who is this shepherd? Psalm 23 says, 'The LORD is my shepherd'. The New Testament unfolds the answer further. Jesus says, 'I am the Good Shepherd' (Jn. 10:11). Jesus actually bases this on this passage from Ezekiel, that's the key to understanding what's being said here. It was a radical thing for Jesus to say 'I am the Good Shepherd.' It shook His hearers to hear Him say those words. At these words, it says, John 10:19, they were divided among themselves. Many were saying, 'He is demon-possessed and raving mad. Why should we listen to Him?' What was it that provoked that kind of reaction to Him saying 'I am the Good Shepherd'? Was He simply saying 'I'm going to be a good leader?' Further on in that chapter, what He said about Himself as the Good Shepherd caused them to pick up stones to throw at Him (Jn. 10:31). They knew perfectly well what He was saying when He said 'I am the Good Shepherd.' It was a very dangerous thing to say, because Herod was king of Judah then, and Jesus is saying there is no true king here at all, I'm the Good Shepherd. But more than that, they knew that when He called Himself the Good Shepherd, He was calling Himself by the title used for God Himself.

Jesus' claim was a massive claim, and even in that tenth chapter of John, He separates Himself from all the other kings and all the other messianic pretenders that have come along. Remember what He said? 'All who came before Me were thieves and robbers – they did not have your interests at heart; they didn't love you the way I love you. They weren't prepared to give their lives for you the way I'm prepared to give My life for you.' The Good Shepherd lays down His life for the sheep, the other shepherds have lain down the sheep's lives for themselves. There were many freedom fighters in Jesus' day, revolutionaries who tried to unite the people behind their goal of driving out the Romans. Many of them arrogated to themselves the title 'the shepherd' and their violent methods got their flock into trouble with the Romans. Many massacres took place as those flocks who were following their shepherd were killed. But Jesus is the tough and tender shepherd of the flock who protects his sheep against dangers from wolves and knows each one by name.

The son of David

When we come to the New Testament, the baby Jesus is dedicated at the temple and the emphasis is that this is great David's greater son. God has fulfilled His promises to the house of David – this child is the successor of David. Jesus comes as David's son. He comes to be the one shepherd who will unite the flock, to use the language of Ezekiel 34. Jesus says there will be one flock and one shepherd (Jn. 10:16). He is the Good Shepherd Who, having secured the ninety-nine in their fold, goes out into the desert looking for the one lost sheep. That's what we're doing in our evangelism. He is the discerning shepherd, Who in the final judgement (again taken right out of Ezekiel 34) will separate the sheep from the goats. And when it comes to his church (1 Pet. 5:4), he is the Chief Shepherd, to Whom all the under-shepherds report. He is the ultimate shepherd-king who fulfils the Davidic covenant as the crowds recognise at his triumphant entry into Jerusalem: 'Hosanna to the son of David!' He is the humble king. There will be a new ruler and that new ruler is Jesus.

There will be a new experience because when He comes, verse 25, he will make a covenant of peace with His flock. In place of all the curses of the Sinai covenant that they'd experienced under the judgement of God – wild animals, drought, famine, the sword – they're now going to experience safety and rain in its season and fruitfulness and peace; '*shalom*' will reign. Now that Hebrew word *shalom*, peace, means much more than just simply the cessation of warfare and the absence of strife. It means a comprehensive state of wholeness and well-being. It suggests a people who are free from fear and insecurity, at peace with themselves. It suggests people who've got a relationship with God where the hostility between them and God is resolved and they're reconciled to God. It also suggests a people who are reconciled with nature. All of that is combined in this idea of *shalom*. It addresses the very things that grip the heart of many people in our world today. Many of us are afraid; of storms, street crime, what other people think, failure, economic downturn, poverty, old age, sickness, bereavement, death. We're insecure people. When the Lord Jesus comes into the world and says, 'I've come to bring peace,' He's saying, 'I've come to deal with those basic fundamental fears and insecurities that lie at the very core of a human being's nature. I've come to bring peace right into the very heart of your life. I've come to speak peace where there is insecurity; I've come to bring peace that the world cannot give and the world cannot take away.' That's why in Ezekiel 34:28, Ezekiel promises when that king comes there will be a day when there will be no fear at any time, no one to make them afraid. The good shepherd defines the measure of the *shalom* (Jn. 10:10): 'I am come that they might have life and that they might have it to the full.' The *shalom* of God is not an activity, an afternoon of undisturbed dozing, it's not boring, there's no need for you to look at your watch when you're enjoying this peace. It is a life where every minute satisfies, every second is worth savouring, where each hour has new pleasures; a life where activity is fulfilling and every sensation brings pleasure.

The new covenant

A new experience and a new experience based upon a new covenant. It was Jeremiah who talked about a new covenant. Here, Ezekiel speaks of a renewed covenant, at the heart of which there is this wonderful promise of God, the Lord is your God, and you are His people. In place of a monarchy divided by sin, God's people united under one shepherd; in place of an undistinguished succession of monarchs, given a single ruler after God's own heart. Now the blessings of this covenant are experienced differently by Christians as opposed to those who lived under the old covenant. One of the things we need to remember in reading the Bible is that in the Old Testament many of the promises of God are put in terms that the people then would understand. For example, the people of God then had a particular relationship to the land in which they lived. It was God's land and they were tenants in God's land, and the fertility of the land was very often a spiritual thermometer, as Chris Wright puts it, of the relationship between Israel and her God. So often the blessings of God are described in terms of the fertility of the land. But under the old covenant, Israel failed miserably in its duties. Time and time again she broke the terms of her relationship to God. Earlier on in Ezekiel, he has talked about Israel as a vine that does not produce the fruit that God is looking for. When the new ruler comes under the new covenant, He says, 'I am the true vine'. The whole message of the New Testament is about the perfect obedience of Christ in our place. Why does He come? He comes to make peace by the blood of His cross, so even though we are covenant breakers by nature, we can have every spiritual blessing in Christ. Through His death on the cross, those who were far away and those who were near are brought together into one new man, all by Christ in this new covenant.

Now but not yet ...

There's the promise of a new ruler, a new experience, and a new covenant, and our experience of this today is partial. The peace we enjoy today is real but it is a partial peace because we still live in a fallen world. We still experience trials of one kind and another, we still know moments of panic and hours of boredom and days when we struggle with pain. Sometimes these are the results of our foolish choices; other times, they're not. Sometimes obedience results in material blessing – sometimes obedience results in persecution, hardship, loss. Yet even here in the midst of sin and trial and temptation, we can experience inexpressible joy because of the nearness of the shepherd. There's this 'already and not yet' aspect to the new covenant. We see the blessings in part though not in fullness. Creation around us still longs for the revelation of the new heaven and the new earth. These light momentary troubles of ours are nothing in comparison to the glory that awaits us in Christ. One day when Christ returns all of this will be gloriously and fully fulfilled as God gathers together His worldwide flock from many nations and brings them into His presence where there will be no more suffering, no more pain, no more disharmony with God or with my neighbour, or even with the world around me.

'The wolf will live with the lamb, the leopard will lie down with the goat, the calf and the lion and the yearling together; and a little child will lead them. The cow will feed with the bear, their young will lie down together; the lion will eat straw like the ox. The infant will play at the hole of the cobra, [and] the young child put his hand into the viper's nest. They will neither harm nor destroy on all my holy mountain, for the earth will be full of the knowledge of the LORD, as the waters cover the sea.' 'For the Lamb at the centre of the throne will be their shepherd; he will lead them to springs of living water. And God will wipe away every tear from their eyes.' Amen.

Can these bones live?
Chapter 36, 37

Introduction

Ezekiel has given us this devastating description of the judgement that was coming on Jerusalem and Judea, and by this time, this judgement has fallen. Everything that Ezekiel had said in such great detail has come to pass. Now he is laying down a picture of great hope for the future. It's the hope of a new leader, who would deal justly with the people and with the world and of a renewed land. But the nation had had good kings before in the past. Since the time of Abraham, the good kings had been followed by bad kings and the people had proved themselves unworthy of the land. So how could they be sure that this time it was going to be any different? That's the big issue that now faces Ezekiel as he addresses the future and the hope of the future.

I had a problem last year with my car. The air conditioning system – which we never needed in Scotland but which we do need in London – broke down, within about five weeks of me getting the car. I went and got it fixed. It broke down within two weeks of being fixed. I went and got it fixed again and it broke down within two weeks of getting fixed. Every time I took it to get it fixed, I wondered, what's going to be different this time? At the beginning of this summer, I had to get it fixed again. This time they took out the whole unit and put a new unit in. It's still working, because it was renewed entirely on the inside.

Here's the promise, a perfect king in a renewed land – with a renewed people. There would be absolutely no point in bringing the people back to the land if they were going to behave in the same old rebellious way. The real issue with Judah and Jerusalem was not one of geography or politics; simply being in the right place and having the right regime wouldn't change anything in ultimate terms. There were many who thought that it would do, just as there are many Christian people who believe that changing society is simply a matter of having the right government in power. What we need to understand is things are worse than we dare believe and the promise of God is greater than we dare hope. Before we can really experience this mighty work of God among us we need to face up again to the depth of our need. It is because we treat sin lightly that we underestimate it and what it will take to transform the situation.

The diagnosis God makes

He says two things about the people (verse 25); firstly, they are defiled and need cleansing. They were ceremonially unclean. It's very hard to take that image of uncleanness and translate it into language that we can understand. The idea of ceremonial uncleanness is familiar to people in other cultures and religious backgrounds – the idea of sacred and profane things. In the ancient world of Israel and the Middle East they understood this whole concept of clean and unclean. Not only were certain things that you ate clean or unclean, but there was a clean land and there were unclean lands. To the Jews especially, the holy land was the holy land, it was a clean land. Everybody outside of the holy land was unclean and therefore under the judgement of God.

They also understood that what was clean could become unclean temporarily or even permanently. You could be unclean from coming into contact with a dead body. What God is saying through Ezekiel, to the people of his day is this: even while they were living in the holy land, they were desecrating it by their behaviour and by their idolatry (25-27). They were turning it into a place of death, making it a place unfit to live in. Instead of staying away from the thing that was defiled, they had become defiled by it (verse 17).

God says the people of God had become unclean. They were acting as if they belonged to the unholy lands of the Gentiles rather than belonging to the holy land of God's people and that's why (verse 19) He was going to scatter them among the Gentile nations. 'You want to live as if you're not God's chosen holy people, then I'll send you out among the unholy, unchosen ones to live the way you really are living!'

They were defiled: how was God's power to be demonstrated? Not only by bringing them back to the land, but also by a total change in their nature. They needed to be redeemed; inwardly, effectively, sprinkled with clean water symbolising radical cleansing from the things that had made the land unclean.

Secondly, they are disobedient and need to be reconciled (36:26,27). The story of Israel from the moment of its rescue from Egypt to its settlement in the Promised Land, right up until Ezekiel's time, is one of constant disobedience to God. We're not sure, the scholars are not sure, whether Israel actually ever implemented the Deuteronomic or Levitical laws. The whole of their history from entering the Promised Land up until being banished from it, in Ezekiel's day, is one of entrenched disobedience to God and so God says He's going to deal radically with this corruption of their hearts.

A new heart

God's diagnosis of the problem is the human heart itself. The heart and the spirit, He says, need to be transformed. In Hebrew the heart is the place where we think, decide and will. The spirit has to do with our inner feelings and aspirations, attitude, disposition and motivation. They needed to think and feel differently. They needed a heart transplant and that's what God promises to do (verse 26): 'I will give you a heart of flesh.' The unyielding, unresponsive stone will be replaced by warm, living, responsive flesh.

Why is God going to cleanse and renew them in their heart? His intention is to produce heart obedience in His people. That will take a creative act on His part (verse 27). The Spirit of God will indwell and recreate them in ways that will change and form their will and their ability to follow God's decrees and to keep God's laws (and that phrase is a direct quotation from Leviticus 26:3, which was God's original intention for them when they came into the Promised Land). God is saying: Look, the people have had time to get their act together and they've failed. But I'm going to do a marvellous, creative work, I'm going to reform them in their hearts. I'm going to bring them back to their land but I'm going to do something even greater than that. I'm going to transform and enable them to do what I've always wanted them to do, to be obedient to My word.

This diagnosis of Israel's and the human condition is straight-forward. They were not just sick any more than we are, in need of some kind of treatment. They were sinners in need of cleansing, rebels in need of reconciliation with their sovereign. They'd made them-selves totally unfit to inhabit God's land and to exist in God's presence. They were offensive to a holy God. Paul in Ephesians 2:3 says about the whole race: 'We are by nature objects of God's wrath.' That was Israel's predicament, and that is our predicament. It's not just simply that we're not making the most of life, not fulfilling our potential as human beings, missing out the spiritual dimension of our humanity: we are under God's judgement. We are under His wrath and we only exist on this planet today because of His commitment to His eternal plan to search out a people for Himself.

You don't have to go far to find the fulfilment of these promises in Ezekiel 36, just to a conversation between Jesus and Nicodemus in John chapter 3. Nicodemus asks Jesus what he should do to inherit eternal life, and Jesus replies, 'No one can enter the kingdom of God unless he is born of water and Spirit.' The cleansing work of the Spirit, bringing together these two images, is straight out of Ezekiel 36. The promise and offer Jesus gives Nicodemus is the same promise and offer we find in verses 25 and 26. You need to be born from above, born anew, says the Lord Jesus. That is the diagnosis God makes. What people need is this radical rebirth. Nothing less than this. Simply modifying the parameters of our lives, re-socialising people so they behave better will not do it. Simply handing someone a list of rules and regulations will certainly not do it. We need radical rebirth. And that is precisely what the good news message of the gospel proclaims.

The means that God uses

The promise of a new leader, a restored land and a renewed people would have been met with scepticism on the part of many people in his day. We've been here before, they would say, what would make this any different? We've had new kings before, and the story always ends in tears. We've had revivals in the land, great high moments of spiritual restoration and renewal, but they didn't change anything. We soon reverted back to type. Why should this be different? So in chapter 37 Ezekiel is transported to Death Valley.

The valley of dry bones

It's a vivid picture of the human predicament from God's perspective. In many ways what we have in this vision in chapter 37 is a dramatic illustration of what has been said in teaching form in chapter 36. The prophet is introduced to a scene of total death. All he sees is a valley of dry bones, the remains of a mighty army scattered in that valley where once earlier in the book he had seen the glory of God. But there's something else: in Middle Eastern culture then, and especially for a Jew, being among the dead would have brought superstitious dread and ritual defilement. Ezekiel, who had trained as a priest, would not want to be anywhere near here. It's as if God is rubbing his nose in it. He makes him walk to and fro through the valley, as if God was saying, 'Make sure you get absolutely defiled by all this.'

This has been the story of Ezekiel's life. One of the clues to Ezekiel is the title 'the son of man' that God uses whenever He speaks to him. One of the costs for Ezekiel was absolute absorption in the will and work of God for his generation. His whole being is invested in the service of God. He even loses his wife half-way through this book. Here he is, as the son of man who's called to serve the will and work of God, utterly defiled, going in and out among these dead people. In all of this, this son of man, Ezekiel, is a great picture of the Son of Man who comes into our world and exposes Himself to all the defilement of our sin for our salvation.

He walks to and fro among them. This is the ultimate picture of despair and hopelessness. That valley of dry bones is where all our plans for the future end up: those years at university, those years invested into your business or career or family or children. It is a hopeless place but it's where we're all going – the place of death, devastation and defilement. The voice of God comes to His servant and says, 'Can these bones live?' Ezekiel doesn't answer God's questions so he bats it right back and says, 'Only You know the answer to that question!'

What can possibly be done for people who are totally hopeless? The New Testament question would be this: What can be done for men and women who are without hope and without God? The people that we are trying to reach for Christ are not simply sick, they are dead before God. This is really where our friends, family members, people we love and pray for are – in the valley of dry bones. What instruments will God use to transform the situation? What will God do to bring life to those dead bones?

Proclamation

First, He will use the word of God and the place of proclamation in this business of making dead bones live. Here's the word that comes to Ezekiel: 'Prophesy to these bones and say to them, "Dry bones, hear the word of the LORD!"' Of all the ridiculous things that we find Ezekiel doing in this book, this has to be the most ridiculous thing he does.

I remember when I first started preaching. I was twelve and my dad took me to see a Billy Graham film. I came back from that film and I used to preach up in the fields behind our house and take these sermons. The sermons were just strings of texts that I put together, but I practised doing that because nobody would let me loose on real people. The cows used to come along and they would 'Moo! Moo!' I got more response from those cows than Ezekiel was going to get from these bones! Actually I got more response from those cows than I've had from some congregations …

I don't know how he started preaching to these bones. Everybody knows that dry bones have no ears to hear, no mind to comprehend, and here is God saying to His servant, 'Preach to the dead! Preach the promise of new life and breath and the knowledge of God!' That is precisely what he does. He preaches the words God has given him to speak. There's no magic rite, no secret incantation, no conjuring trick – it's just plain, simple straightforward preaching. It's the preaching that makes the difference.

Here is a situation that confronts every Christian missionary, every Christian evangelist. It's not simply that we're up against spiritual apathy or hostility. It's not simply that we're striving all the time to make our message relevant and contemporary – we have to listen to the world as well as listen to the word – it's much worse than that. The New Testament uses this picture of Ezekiel to describe people all over the world, whether they're Jews or Gentiles: You were dead, it says, in trespasses and sins. Getting people to believe our message is not simply hard, it's impossible. Unless we start from that premise, we're going to be in all kinds of frustration and disappointment. It is impossible to bring people to faith in Jesus Christ ourselves. Nothing we can do can make it any easier – it's a graveyard. What are we to do in the circumstances? If new life is going to happen in our nation it is through preaching that it's going to happen. God has promised that He will bless the preaching of His word however ridiculous it is – and it is.

What was he to preach? He was to preach the word of the Lord that has the power to change things. In the New Testament this word is the message of Christ crucified which Paul says is both the power and the wisdom of God. Just expressing opinions, passing on speculations, will not make any difference. Subtracting the bits that people don't like so that what you're communicating are the positive spins on the Christian message will not do it. I know what kind of disciples you get if you leave out judgement and wrath and don't speak of the cross as the substitutionary death of Jesus in the place of sinners.

Visualise the scene. The preacher starts to preach and something begins to happen. You remember the song? 'Dem bones, dem bones, dem dry bones … hear the word of the Lord!' That's what going on here. All the bits and pieces are coming together and there's a clanking and a banging sound. All these skeletons are marching around, looking for something to put on and the skin begins to cover all the skeletons. There they are, a mighty army that are being resurrected by the power of the word of God. The word of God is living and active and sharper than any two-edged sword. Believe it.

The word and the Spirit

I want you to notice the preaching of the word of God, and the action of the Spirit of God together accomplish resurrection. The Hebrew word for breath, wind and spirit are all the same word, *ruach*. In Genesis 1 we see the Spirit of God like a mighty gale, rushing over the face of the unformed earth, bringing form and life. Genesis 1 again, it's the Spirit who breathes into human beings the breath of life. In Ezekiel, it is the word of God that releases the recreating Spirit to resurrect this vast army. Jesus, in John 3, brings together the work of the Spirit in the new birth and He likens it to the mysterious working of a mighty wind. By preaching the word of God, Ezekiel is not only proclaiming truthfully what God has said but he is also creating the context into which the Spirit of God will gladly and powerfully come. The proclamation of the word of God creates the context into which the Holy Spirit is happy to move in power to do His resurrection work in these people's lives.

Prayer and proclamation belong together. These are the two basic components of church life; one without the other is deficient. The early church leaders devoted themselves to prayer and the ministry of the word. We believe in the sovereignty of God but we also believe that God has ordained the means by which He is prepared to act in this world. He has given us His orders to proclaim His word and call on His name. Jesus said, 'The words that I speak to you, they are spirit and they are life.' He could say to His disciples, again taking the themes right from this passage: 'You are clean through the word I have spoken to you.' Martin Luther said, 'God's word will keep you from

sin, or sin will keep you from God's word.' Jesus tells Nicodemus that
he needs to be born again by the water and the Spirit, the cleansing
ministry of the Spirit through the word that renews.

The real secret of spiritual life for our churches and our nation lies
in the word and in the Spirit, by proclamation and prayer. What was
it that renewed the lives of those Corinthians? Paul says, I came to you
in weakness and fear, and with much trembling, but, he says, I came
proclaiming the word that God had given to me, the testimony about
God. I came preaching Jesus Christ and Him crucified. 'My message
and my preaching were not with wise and persuasive words but with
a demonstration of the Spirit's power.' What was the effect of this
preaching and proclamation?

Here's the kind of people that made up the church in Corinth
– 'the sexually immoral, idolaters, adulterers, male prostitutes, homo-
sexual offenders, thieves, the greedy, drunkards, slanderers, swindlers'
(1 Cor. 6:9,10). But they've been transformed by the word of Christ.
They weren't that any more, they'd been transformed; they'd stopped
doing those things that were wrong and they were now going in a different direction. It is the word of God he preached that caused this to
happen. 'You were washed, you were sanctified, you were justified in
the name of the Lord Jesus Christ and by the Spirit of God.' It comes
straight out of Ezekiel; the cleansing, the washing, the renewal of the
Holy Spirit and the word of God that Paul speaks about when he's
describing that amazing work that God had accomplished in his people in Titus 3. He speaks of the same cleansing and renewal of the
Holy Spirit: 'He saved us through the washing of rebirth, renewal by
the Holy Spirit whom He poured out on us generously through Jesus
Christ our Saviour'.

The work God accomplishes

What is the work God accomplishes? It's two-fold. First He renews
the life of His people. We have to stand back a bit from this prophecy
and ask ourselves how and where has this prophecy been fulfilled? It's
been fulfilled, as many Old Testament prophecies have, at various

levels. There is no doubt the first is the level of the return of the exiled Jews to Jerusalem. They did come back to their land. They did experience spiritual renewal. It was during the exile that synagogue worship and preaching as we know it was born in their communities and when they eventually came back under Ezra and Nehemiah, they were a humbled people, purified by suffering. They rebuilt the city and the temple; they reclaimed the land in response to the prayers of people like Daniel and the preaching ministry of people like Ezra. Yet we sense an inadequacy because we know that though they came back, it wasn't a long-lasting work. And so the primary level at which this prophecy is fulfilled is Pentecost, for Pentecost initiates the age of the Spirit. There the Spirit of God becomes an indwelling presence in the heart of the individual believer, when the believers were altogether in the upper room, joined constantly in prayer. The Spirit flowed and moved mightily as Peter proclaims that first Christian message and since Pentecost the same Spirit of God has been at work everywhere in the world bringing radical cleansing and renewed life to men and women.

We are told in chapter 36 of Ezekiel that these renewed people are ashamed and disgraced over their conduct. Repentance is one of the side effects of this work of the Spirit. In an age that idolises self-esteem, this may sound strange. But as we grow in our appreciation of the good news message, we do not view ourselves in a better light. Rather we see ourselves as the chief of sinners, but we also grow in our understanding that though we are far worse than we ever could have imagined, we are more loved than we ever dreamed possible.

Revival

The prophecy is fulfilled primarily at Pentecost. The prophecy has also been fulfilled at various points in church history when God has visited His people at periods that we call revival. The Spirit of God has stirred up people to pray and then flowing from prayer and the proclamation of the word, a whole community has been transformed by the word and Spirit of God. Preachers like Whitefield and Wesley proclaimed the word of God in ways that aroused a sleeping church and brought to life thousands upon thousands of those who were dead in sin. We must still pray that perhaps in our day God would do something that would shake His church to life; where the preachers of the gospel would be heard not simply by the sheep so that they rearrange themselves into different flocks, depending on who is the flavour of the month, but that the world outside would hear this message and that those men and women who are today dead in sin would hear the word of life and would come in their thousands to faith in our Saviour.

I believe the prophecy is yet to be fulfilled with respect to Israel, the ongoing people of God. As yet their hearts are still hard, they're not a gospel people. They still demonstrate that essential rebellion against God and in their arrogance disregard the good news message of Jesus. In New Testament language, a hardening has happened to Israel but that is not a final hardening. The apostle Paul suggests a day is coming when the fullness of the Gentiles have come in, when God's mercy will yet again be directed towards His ancient people and they will experience this new birth that we have experienced, and on that day their hard hearts will be replaced with hearts of flesh. Can you imagine the consequences for worldwide evangelism of God's recapturing His ancient people and transforming them by the gospel? The prophecy is going to be ultimately fulfilled. Do you remember Jesus, on one occasion after resurrecting a dead man in a cemetery, said, 'There is a coming a day when the voice of the Son of Man' (echoes of Ezekiel) 'will be heard and the dead who are lying in their graves will be raised.' God's wonderful plan includes bringing us to heaven and making us perfect both in body and soul when Jesus returns.

The honour of His name

Lastly he restores the honour of His name (36:14 – 37:28). The whole emphasis is on people knowing that 'I the LORD have done this, I the LORD have spoken, I the LORD have done it'. Up till now His name had been defiled among the nations as people had said, 'What kind of God is He? Look at these devastated people, dispossessed of their land, what kind of God is the God of Israel that this should happen? He must be a weak God. Our gods, the gods of Babylon and Egypt, are powerful gods; the God of Israel is a weak God.' But God says, 'I'm going to do this work. One of the main effects of that work is that the Gentile nations are going to see that I have done it.' And chapter 37 ends with an emphasis that there is only one way of salvation for the whole world, one way of salvation for Jews and Gentiles; one shepherd, for everybody, whatever their background is, one ruler, one flock. All this is good news, not just for the people but for the Lord Himself. The crucifixion, resurrection and then exaltation of His Son, the miracle of the new birth in countless lives; the future conversion of the Jews and the ultimate resurrection of the dead, will in the long run vindicate His name among the nations. The act of salvation through Jesus Christ will, at the end of history, be the very thing that brings greatest glory to God and that ought not to surprise us for there's nothing higher than this. For God to delight in His own perfections is entirely appropriate but to delight in anything less would be idolatry for Him. The exaltation of God is the great end of salvation as well as creation.

> 'Then you will know on that day when many shall come from north and south and east and west and sit down at the table with Abraham and Isaac and Jacob, on that day, then you will know that I the Lord have spoken, and I have done it', says the Lord Almighty.

Amen.

A river runs through it
Chapters 40 – 48

Introduction

Some years ago, we had a fairly large staff team in the church and somebody had the idea that we weren't working together as we might do. They brought in these experts to help us work effectively as a team. It was very helpful. We found out what kind of people we were and how we operated. There were team players and then those who were the pastoral people. If they had an appointment, they were likely to be late because they'd met someone, which really frustrated the co-ordinator/completer types. They got frustrated by everything and everybody because they worked to schedules and needed to know exactly where everybody was, and had to have lots of meetings ... and I do admire them. One individual came out as a shaper, who sees the big picture, comes up with a bright idea, and expects everyone to know by osmosis what the idea is and to catch up in their own time. I came into that last category and was frustrating all the co-ordinator/completer types, people types and team players. Just discovering what we were helped us to work more effectively together.

Ezekiel is a co-ordinator/completer type. He's fascinated with detail. In this last section he is detailing the final temple and the splitting up of the land into various categories. Let me put this last section into the big picture of the second part of Ezekiel's book. Having vindicated his prophetic ministry, because all that he had predicted had come true, he is now looking into the future. In chapters 38 and 39 he describes the final conflict, the birth pains of a new creation, and shows us that history is littered with people, with powers both human and demonic, that are aimed against God's people but God will be finally and ultimately victorious over them all.

Now in chapters 40 to 48, he sees a visionary re-ordering of an entire new world, centred around the temple of God. It's a new kind of temple, with radically raised standards of holiness demanded of those who serve and worship in it and a radically new focus on sacrifice. That is almost its defining thing.

Notice the date he tells us: 'In the twenty-fifth year of our exile, at the beginning of the year, on the tenth of the month, in the fourteenth year after the fall of the city' ... There is no doubt, from another reference (46:17) that he is putting this figure in, twenty-five, and mentioning it is at the beginning of the year because he is flagging up to those reading his book that they are half-way towards the year of Jubilee. Every fifty years in the history of the people of Israel they celebrated a year of Jubilee on the tenth day of the seventh month. Slaves were released, the land liberated from bondage and so on. The year of Jubilee becomes the great picture of the salvation, the final vindication of God. He is saying, by signalling this in chapter 40 verse 1, we are half-way to the year of Jubilee. Here is a description of heaven from half-way there. Speaking, writing and prophesying to people faced with the reality of the absence of God, he is telling them what it will be like when God is present in all His fullness, might and power.

Ezekiel's vision

Ezekiel is speaking in a vision. He is not having a kind of videotaped replay of something that is still to come; this is a vision. When you read of a vision, in these apocalyptic books in the Old Testament or in the New Testament, don't take your newspaper to understand it. Take your Bible, because the symbolism, metaphors and concepts don't come from your newspaper, they come from the Bible. You need to interpret a vision, not visualise a vision, and that's very important as we come to understanding what is being said here.

I'm concerned to interpret what this last section is about. He is telling us, first of all, that in this future day that is to come, God is present with His people. They're in exile in a far off land, with their temple destroyed, their city devastated, their people deported. They needed to hear that there was a day coming when God would be present with His people. So he tells us (chapter 40) that he was set on a very high mountain. There is no very high mountain but he is speaking here not about literal geography but theological geography. Moses had gone up to Mount Nebo and was allowed to see the Promised Land. Ezekiel is taken to a very high mountain and enabled to see the ultimate Promised Land, heaven itself. He is using theological language as he describes the final temple. The valley that he had seen earlier, Death Valley, has now been raised up to a great pinnacle above all the mountains of the world and on it, the temple of God is going to be established. Out of the resurrection life that He is going to breathe into people by His word and His Spirit, He is going to build this temple.

God is present with His people

The heart of the message about the temple is that God is present with His people. The description of the temple finds its culmination in chapter 43 when the glory comes back into it. That's important for Ezekiel. Earlier in this book (chapter 11) he had been taken to the temple in a vision, and there he had seen the glory of God departing from the Holy of Holies. In chapters 40 to 48 we have a new temple and a new city with the name 'The LORD is there' because the glory comes back from the east, through the eastern door of the temple, right into the Holy of Holies, to be present with God's people again.

This idea of the temple is tied into the history of redemption. It is rich in symbolism. The temple actually had two functions. First of all it pointed to the presence of God among His people. The God who marched before Israel through the desert now lives with them on His holy hill. Of course, they never ever believed that God's presence was tied to any local spot geographically. When the magnificent temple of Solomon was being consecrated and Solomon was praying the prayer of consecration for the temple, just before the glory cloud, the Shekinah, comes to fill the Holy of Holies at the very centre of the temple, Solomon says 'this God that we worship does not dwell in a temple made with hands.' Ezekiel has been shown the very same thing, that the glory of God is present where His people are. While the temple represented the presence of God, it never limited the presence of God, for He was present in the midst of His people.

The gate of God

The second function of the temple was to be the gate of God, because it was through the temple that people had access to God. The temple spoke about a way of access but it also spoke about all the things that keep us out of the presence of God. There were all kinds of obstacles that kept all kinds of people at a distance; Gentiles couldn't get into the compound at all. Women could get so far in, men a bit further, priests a little bit further and then only the high priest once a year was able to get right into the Holy of Holies. The temple emphasised the barrier of sin that keeps men away from God. Even those who served in the temple, the priests, were reminded all the time that they were unclean and needed God's cleansing. So the temple reminded people of the barriers that keep us away from God. God is holy, we are unholy.

The temple was also given to people as a means of teaching the way of access to God who is holy – the way of sacrifice. That is why many times a day, people brought their sacrifices to be offered on the altar as a reminder, this holy God is only approachable by way of a sacrifice that has to be made for sin. So the temple, then, is both a barrier and an avenue. It systematically excluded various groups, kept others at a distance, but at the same time, it offered a way for people to come to know God.

Israel in exile was to discover, largely through Ezekiel's ministry, that God was still present with them even in a foreign land. If the temple stands for the presence of God, then when God's glory moves out to Babylon where they are, they discovered a lesson that is important for us to grasp. If the temple represents the presence of God among His people, when the glory leaves that physical building and goes to where His people are, they're learning that the temple is where they are and where the glory rests. They are learning that the indestructible temple is the presence of God in glory among and with His people, wherever His people find themselves (11:16).

The real temple

The New Testament tells us that the earthly temple only ever had a symbolic significance. The literal temple, the real temple, was the one in heaven. The one on earth was a visual aid, a shadow of the real thing. There is a true tabernacle set up by the Lord, not by man; the earthly priests 'serve at a sanctuary that is a copy and shadow of what is in heaven' (Heb. 8:5). 'When Christ came as high priest of the good things that are already here, He went through the greater and more perfect tabernacle that is not man-made, that is to say, not a part of this creation' (Heb. 9:11). 'It was necessary, then, for the copies of the heavenly things to be purified with these sacrifices, but the heavenly things themselves with better sacrifices than these'(Heb. 9:23) to purify them. Ezekiel is describing a perfect temple. Interestingly, when the exiles went back to the Promised Land and rebuilt their temple, they didn't follow Ezekiel's pattern at all. He is describing the heavenly sanctuary.

How does the New Testament help us to interpret this temple image, especially the two ideas of the presence of God and the gate of God? Where in the New Testament do you find God present with His people and the way to God clearly explained? Where do you find the glory of God resting in the New Testament? Malachi was to promise, 'Then suddenly the Lord you are looking for will come into His temple.' Luke's gospel begins in the temple with the announcement of the coming of Christ and Jesus being brought in for dedication into the temple. As Jesus is held in the hands of Simeon, He is described as the glory of His people Israel. The temple is often described in those terms, 'the glory of His people, Israel' – this boy is the glory of His people, Israel. Where do you see the temple of God in the New Testament? Where is the radiance of God's glory and the exact representation of His being? John says, 'We have seen His glory, the glory of the One and Only [Son] who came from the Father, full of grace and truth' (Jn. 1:14).

When you come to the New Testament, look at the ministry of our Lord Jesus, and what do you find Him doing? Once at the beginning and once at the end of the New Testament, you find the Lord Jesus Himself, going in through the eastern gate, through the eastern door of the temple, right into the very courtyard of the temple. By His great sign action, He suspends the worship of God in the temple. When He is whipping out those people, He is not just fighting against injustice; He is not simply making a statement against those people in the temple who are ripping off those tourists who were coming to offer their worship to God. He is bringing a halt to the way in which the temple did its business. You couldn't offer sacrifices in the temple unless you bought them from some of the temple traders and you couldn't buy them unless you changed your money into the temple currency. When Jesus throws all their tables over, chases out all the animals and causes absolute upheaval everywhere in the temple, temporarily He is suspending the process of offering sacrifices. He does it twice: no wonder they wanted to kill Him.

In John 2, this leads to a big discussion among the people about Who Jesus is. They're angry about what He has done and say, 'Show us a sign.' He says, 'I'll give you a sign. Destroy this temple and I will raise it in three days.' Thinking He meant a building, they said, 'It has taken forty-six years for us to build this temple and you're going to raise it in three days?' John adds the comments, 'But the temple He spoke of was His body.' The final temple is the temple of His own flesh, and whereas in the earthly temple, the temple bread was reserved only for the sons of Levi, Jesus breaks the bread and distributes it to all who follow Him. Again, with a temple reference. He says,

'The stone the builders rejected has become the capstone. This is the Lord's doing and it is marvellous in our eyes.' So the temple made without hands is the only authentic dwelling place for the glory of God. 'In Christ all the fullness of the deity lives in bodily form.' No wonder Jesus could say, referring to the building, 'I tell you that one greater than the temple is here.' God is present with His people. You cannot read Ezekiel's description of that perfectly holy temple, without using your New Testament to tell you that God's final perfect temple is Jesus.

God is accessible to His people

This is the second thing that is emphasised in Ezekiel. We find in Ezekiel (42:13 – 44:4) that God does not dwell in unapproachable holiness alone. He has created this temple as a place in which He can have fellowship with a cleansed people and where a holy people have perfect fellowship in His holy presence and engage in holy worship. That is one of the great emphases of this book and the stress is that God is accessible in this temple. The temple is the place where God is present. If in your mind you're thinking of the use that Paul makes of the expression, 'in Christ', then you will not be far off. Here's a lovely picture of what it means to be in Christ. If Christ is the building and you're in the building and there are big walls now around this building to keep you from ever falling out again or being banished again, or even for God ever getting out and leaving again, what a great picture this is of the security, the safety and the enjoyment we have in Christ.

In Christ

In Christ, God is accessible to His people. The climax is this massive altar, bigger than the altar described in the Levitical description (42:13 – 44:4), bigger than the altar they built when they built the renewed temple. It dominates the sanctuary. Here are offerings that actually work, that are effective in cleansing from sin so we're acceptable to God (43:27). I imagine one of the questions in the people's minds was this: 'God is back in His temple, but will He have us back? We've been rebellious.' Ezekiel says yes, in this temple you've access to God. 'I will accept you,' says the Lord. The altar is the place that actualises the welcome. God has not come back to His temple simply to bask in the surroundings of this lovely new building. He has come back to a fellowship with humans. The days of His wrath are past. He reaches out to us with acceptance. The grace of God has transformed this place of defilement and betrayal to a place of acceptance and reconciliation. Isn't that what it means to be in Christ? A new creation – the old has gone, the new has come! The altar is at the centre of it. For only by sacrifice can this reconciliation and acceptance take place. Hebrews says the only way the heavenly sanctuary can be purified is by the shedding of blood. He emphasises that it is impossible that the blood of bulls and goats could take away sin. You see, even in the Old Testament, already you have these indicators that the sacrificial system just wasn't cutting it as far as the relationship with God was concerned. It couldn't help you if you'd committed a deliberate sin. Psalm 51 indicates that sacrifices only went so far, they didn't help you if you'd committed murder or adultery. But these sacrifices make us entirely acceptable to God.

We can't read the Old Testament without our New Testaments. What sacrifice makes us absolutely acceptable to God? There is only one sacrifice for all time, the sacrifice of our Lord Jesus. No wonder Ezekiel is stretching his language, going into such detail here. He is speaking in language only he understands as a priest; he understood temples and sacrifices; he's saying there's coming a day when sacrifices will accomplish something that goes beyond any of our power to imagine and will guarantee an abiding presence in God's presence. We have that confidence today. 'Therefore, brothers, since we have confidence to enter the Most Holy Place by the blood of Jesus, by a new and living way opened for us through the curtain, that is, His body, and since we have a great priest over the house of God, let us draw near to God with a sincere heart in full assurance of faith' (Heb. 10:19-22). That's what makes God accessible to us today.

The living water

In Christ that heavenly temple, a river flows there. The prophet Joel spoke of a day when a fountain shall flow from the Lord's house. Zechariah said, 'On that day living water will flow from Jerusalem.' A river flows from the south side of the temple – that's the place of sacrifice. Wherever the river flows there is life. You're going to hear that image again, used by the final temple Himself. When He's sitting by the well with one of those who's excluded from the temple because she is a Samaritan, offering her a way in which she can worship God, right there, He says, 'If only you'll recognise who I am, I'll give you streams of living water that will satisfy you for ever more.'

Remember John 7, on the great day of the Feast, Jesus goes into the temple and makes this grand announcement: 'If anyone is thirsty, let him come to Me and drink. Whoever believes in Me, as the Scripture has said, streams of living water shall flow from within him' (Jn. 7:37,38). Where that temple is, there the river flows. In Revelation 22, the Lamb is there amongst His people and God is there with them, and we read the river of the water of life, as clear as crystal, was flowing from the throne of God and of the Lamb. Ezekiel says where that river flows, everything will live. 'I am come,' says Jesus, 'that you might have life, and that you might have life to the full.' There is a river there, that brings life and healing to the nations, says Revelation, healing to people who are broken by sin. Whatever background you may have come from, the healing that you need is in Christ Jesus. Come to Christ and have that river well up from inside you. We're in that final temple. God is accessible to His people.

God is honoured among His people

There's one last thing for us to note in that final temple (43:13 – 46:24), where the restoration of the worship of God takes place. Ezekiel describes what's inside this great temple, with its massive walls. It's a reformed temple priesthood and a reformed worship. Again this has a New Testament relevance to us. For whereas under the old covenant the people were separated from the priesthood, what is the great declaration we have in the New Testament of the people of God? The great principle, rediscovered at the time of the Reformation, is of the priesthood of all believers. What does John say in Revelation? He says you are a kingdom of priests to serve our God. What does Peter say (1 Pet. 2:9)? You were once nothing but now 'you are chosen people, a royal priesthood, a holy nation.' Later on in the New Testament, we see a God-centred community, a holy people in a holy place and that's what we have here in Ezekiel as well.

Consider the New Testament teaching that the believer and the church are now a temple because they are in Christ. And because we are in Christ, serving Him as a priesthood, we are to offer our Lord Jesus living sacrifices. It's the language of liturgy, that's the Greek word that's used. That's the word that's used in Romans 12 verses 1 and 2. When we give our generous gifts to God's work, what are they? They are a fragrant offering, an acceptable sacrifice, pleasing to God. When we stand together and sing our songs of enthusiastic celebration for what God has done, what are we doing? We're offering Him a sacrifice of praise. Where is the church built (Eph. 2)? It's built on the foundation of the apostles and the prophets with Christ Himself as the chief cornerstone; that's the language of a temple. 'In Him the whole building is joined together and rises to become a holy temple in the Lord. And in Him you too are being built together to become a dwelling in which God lives by His Spirit.' It's straight from Ezekiel. Or 'As you come to Him, the living Stone – rejected by men but chosen by God and precious to Him – you also, like living stones, are being built into a spiritual house to be a holy priesthood, offering spiritual sacrifices acceptable to God through Jesus Christ' (1 Pet. 2:4,5).

Holiness

One of the great emphases that Ezekiel lays in these last chapters is on holiness. Those of us who are Christians indwelt by the Holy Spirit are called to holiness. Paul argues. 'What agreement is there between the temple of God and idols? For we are the temple of the living God. As God says, "I will live with them and walk among them, and I will be their God, and they will be My people. Therefore don't touch the unclean thing."' Ezekiel 37:26 has come true. 'I will put my sanctuary among them for ever. My dwelling-place will be with them; I will be their God and they will be My people. [Then] the nations will know that I the LORD make Israel holy, when My sanctuary is among them.'

A new heaven

This section of Ezekiel ends where it begins, if you look back at chapter 40 for a second. 'In visions of God He took me to the land of Israel and set me up on a very high mountain, on whose south side were some buildings that looked like a city.' In chapter 48 he picks up that city metaphor again as he talks about the land that is the inheritance of his people. Every tribe has a portion. All the people of God have a place in this land. Everybody has an apportioned place, an allotted space, in this heaven that Ezekiel is describing.

Remember the language that Jesus uses in Matthew 5 as He quotes from Psalm 37 verse 11, which says 'The meek will inherit the land and enjoy great peace.' Jesus says they will inherit the earth; literally, the land. Right now we don't have the land, we're still aliens and strangers. 'Here we do not have an enduring city, but we are looking for one that is above' (Heb.13:14). That's where we are today. In that city there will be a place for you. Ezekiel 48 is saying there's a place for everybody. Your place is measured out. 'I go to prepare a specific place for you,' Jesus said. That's what heaven is. It's the place allotted for us, our inheritance.

The book of Revelation picks up so much of the imagery and metaphors of Ezekiel that in many ways you cannot understand Revelation without reading Ezekiel. Nor can you understand Ezekiel without reading Revelation. One of the keys to understanding Revelation is to see it as a description of that heavenly temple, so in chapter 1 you find the Lord Jesus enthroned and exalted and where is He? He's in that outer bit just outside the Holy of Holies and He's standing next to the seven-branched candlestick that represents the churches. Then you see the Lord Jesus going up through the curtain into the Holy of Holies and sitting on the seat, the throne of God Himself, where the ark of the covenant was. He goes there as the sacrifice that has just been made. Revelation 5:6 – a Lamb that has just been slain enters. He is worthy and comes and sits down upon the throne, the object of heaven's worship. Go to chapter 8, you see the laver in which they cleansed themselves – the book of Revelation is built around the imagery of that heavenly sanctuary. There you see who the perfect sacrifice is, the Lamb whose blood cleanses from all sin. There you see who sits upon the throne of God. It is the Lamb who is in the midst of them and He is called their shepherd; that's what Ezekiel had predicted.

There in the book of Revelation we come to that climactic view: a new Jerusalem, a new city, where all the people of God are from the old covenant and the new covenant because the names of the apostles as well as the prophets are written on the foundations and walls of the city. All of God's people are there. There's only one difference. John says, 'I did not see a temple in the city, because the Lord God Almighty and the Lamb are its temple.' There is your definitive New Testament explanation of Ezekiel's vision. The Lord God Almighty and the Lamb are its temple. The entire city has become one giant holy place, and there's no altar there, because the Lamb, the One Who's made the sacrifice, is at the very heart of that new Jerusalem. Everybody who's there has got in there because of the sacrifice He has made on their behalf on the cross. Only the city remains and His servants serve him day and night. People from every tribe and nation come and gather there. Ezekiel's last words at the end of chapter 48 are to give a description of that city – he says, 'The LORD is there'. Our Bible-believing New Testament minds hear the message that was sounded loudly in the ear of the apostle John when he cried out, 'Now the dwelling of God is with men and He will live with them. They will be His people – He will be their God.' When you read Ezekiel, you see a vision of heaven from half-way there. That is our destiny. Beloved, our destiny is to belong to that perfect place, to be a perfect people, to enjoy perfect pleasures for ever more. John Bunyan describes it in his book, the *Pilgrim's Progress* as he sees Christian and

Hopeful safely across the river, into the celestial city. There are many who are gathered there waiting to greet them and he adds this little comment: 'I wished myself to be among them'. To be there, to be with Christ, is by far the best. Thanks be to God.

The Addresses

Manifesto of the King

by Peter Lewis

PETER LEWIS

Peter has led the Cornerstone Church, Nottingham, since 1969. In that time it has grown from fifty people to five hundred, with a full time staff of six at home and about twenty abroad. Peter has served on the Theological Commission of the World Evangelical Fellowship and the Council of Management of the Evangelical Alliance. He travels extensively and has twice been a speaker at Keswick in Grand Cayman in the Caribbean! Peter is married to Valerie and they have two sons. They both enjoy classical music, long walks and plenty to read.

Manifesto of the King
Matthew 5:1 – 16

The subject I've been given tonight is the community of the King. Community is the key word and I'm going to speaking on that in the light of the Beatitudes: 'Blessed are the poor in spirit, for theirs is the kingdom of heaven. Blessed are those who mourn, for they will be comforted. Blessed are the meek, for they will inherit the earth.'

What a revolutionary manifesto this is in all in aspects; in the Lord it exalts, the faith it proclaims, and the people it creates. The world says, 'Blessed are the loud, the proud.' Jesus says, 'Blessed are the poor in spirit.' The world says, 'Blessed are those who hedge their bets and spread their portfolios.' Jesus says, 'Blessed are the pure in heart, for they shall see God.' But let's never forget that the Lord Jesus is speaking of people, not simply principles; of flesh and blood and realities, and not merely nice ideas. Remember that He's speaking about His people in community as well as in their private lives. That's clear from the famous picture of the city set on a hill which can't be hidden. 'You are the light of the world.' 'You' is plural. You are the light of the world; a city on a hill cannot be hidden. A city isn't a single house but many houses and a community of people. It's of the church as a

revolutionary people living in revolutionary communities that I want
to speak.

People in community

It's interesting that the pictures we have of the church in the Bible are
so often pictures of people in community. We are an elect people, a
victorious army, the city of God, the temple of God, the family of
God, the body of Christ. Notice the stress on community: army, city,
family, body, with the corresponding implications of belonging to one
another, relying on one another, fulfilling one another. The concept of
the church takes two forms in the New Testament; the universal
church and the local church. Most of the references to the church in
the New Testament actually are references to the church in a particular place. That stops us from having too mystical a concept of the
church and avoiding the concrete flesh and blood realities of church
life. If a person says, 'I belong to the church,' I have good reason to say:
'Which church? Where?' The apostle Paul preached, baptised and
gathered communities. They had form, structure, authority and discipline, although I don't want to give the impression they were army
camps, any more than they were holiday camps. When the Lord Jesus
sent His gospel out into the world by the mouths of the apostles
and many others, He didn't simply put people right with God as
individuals. He gathered them into communities called churches;
community is at the heart of the reality.

Christian churches, however, are not simply another variation on
human communities. They are the communities of the kingdom, communities whose people have in common a new life and a new Lordship;
new priorities and new goals. They are a people bound together by a
common faith and motivated by a common love. Jesus here describes us
as the community of the Beatitudes, communities of the poor in spirit,
the meek, the merciful, the hungry for righteousness, and the pure in
heart, the peacemakers, those who are often persecuted for righteous-
ness-sake and those who mourn for the brokenness of the world. I can
imagine someone saying, 'My church isn't like that.' But can you say that

these things are valued in your community? 'Yes.' Can you say that in your community the sins which are the contradiction of these things are confessed? 'Yes.' Can you say that you and your fellow worshippers pray to be more like this description that we have in the Beatitudes? 'I suppose so.' Then can it be that these things really are there, at home as well as at Keswick? They may be buried under the limitations and preoccupations of human life but they're growing upward, seeking the light, straining against blockages and by the Spirit's care and work they can come to visibility and maturity. If so, then yours too is the community of the Beatitudes, just as Jesus said it was.

The Sermon on the Mount isn't simply a prescription, it's actually a description of a reality guaranteed and sustained in the world by the power and the goodness of God. It's not a prescription of society, a kind of socialist utopia. No parliament can legislate for this, and no amount of education, technical or moral, can achieve it. This is not a new initiative but God's new society, a new kind of humanity, with a new kind of life working within them. It's a kingdom where people pray for their enemies and love the outsider; where people are salt in the politics of life, and light in the darkness and loneliness of the world. They are the people of the kingdom in whom God the Holy Spirit is at work, healing a broken world and saving a lost one.

Working together

Furthermore, the Beatitudes don't describe different people as if some in the kingdom of God were poor in spirit and others hungry for righteousness and others pure in heart and others meek and so on – no, they are meant to be taken together. All these things are at the heart of the life of the kingdom, and the life of the kingdom is the new life that is at work within each one of us. The Beatitudes do not describe the Lord's elite in the churches but all the Lord's people in the churches. You may be a young Christian or an old one, an easy person or a rather difficult one, a person who finds some of these very much easier to live out than others. I was delighted with a misprint that appeared two or three years ago in the Christian business pages, which listed one entry as: The Little Bothers of the Good Shepherd, 27 Thornley Street, Wolverhampton. We are very different people in our communities and those differences can be both bothersome and necessary. You know how it is back home; how it is in all the churches. Some people are by nature the accelerator – desperately wanting to go at one hundred miles an hour without being too concerned about the direction taken. Some people are the brakes, always trying to slow everything down, sometimes keen on getting into the nearest lay-by for a generation or two. Some people are the steering wheel, studying the terrain with great concentration and anxiously keeping the car on the road, negotiating the bends and the potholes immediately ahead with care and skill. We need all of these at different times. But what good are the accelerator, the brakes and the steering wheel in a car without a working engine? Such is a church without the power of the Holy Spirit – a rusting hulk on the side of the road, an eyesore and an anomaly. But when the Spirit is there, the Spirit of love, joy, peace, long suffering, gentleness, goodness, faith, meekness, self-control – then we are going to heaven in style! And there's always plenty of room in the back for those who want to make the journey with us.

The work of the Spirit

The chief point is that we have the Holy Spirit at work in our lives to make us more like our Saviour. The Spirit's great work is to conform us to Christ, to deepen the family likeness in each one of us. As we pray in our churches, serve in our world, read our Bibles and love one another, that family likeness will become more and more clear. A personal walk with God will always affect your relationships with other believers and they in turn will affect you, because they too have the life of the kingdom within them. That's why we can see each of these Beatitudes in community or social terms; they remove the blocks and help bind us together in this strange and wonderful new life that we have in Christ. We see our sins and become less proud than we were. We see God our Father in the beauty of holiness and His supreme majesty and it's easy to mourn the sins of our own lives and our sinful world. We see the grace of Christ and tend to become, little by little, more meek and gentle with others. We see the eternal goal before us and become more single-minded about God, which incidentally is what the Greek phrase 'pure in heart' really means.

The people of God in their communities are a people drawn together by a great grace, and kept together by a passionate commitment. 'Hear, O Israel, the Lord your God, the Lord is one. Love the Lord your God with all your heart and with all your soul and with all your strength.' God Himself is the model of that love in His own uttermost love for us. The love that meets the extravagant love of God with its own fledgling extravagance in praise and prayer is the love that not only reaches up to the God it has not yet seen but also reaches out to the brother or sister that it has seen. In this way, the churches become the likeness of Christ in the world. In our church communities, we live out something of the life of God that we cannot live out on our own. God has lived in community from all eternity, in the community of the Father, the Son and the Holy Spirit. It's in our varied grace as community that we more fully bear the image of Jesus Christ who alone has all the perfections.

The whole people of God

John Stott has said, it needs the whole people of God to understand the whole love of God. May we not also say in some ways, it needs the whole people of God to be the whole image of God. As such, we'll also be a people under attack from Satan, who hates that image, and especially under attack as communities. We can't hope to survive that attack by giving up the church and becoming 'lone rangers'. We'll only be the more easily picked off. We need each other to survive and to flourish, but the great temptation and attack of the enemy is always in the area of relationships. Satan uses distance and difference; he fosters indifference, neglect, dislike, suspicion, fear, irritation, contempt, resentment and so he weakens us as churches. Why do such things weaken us? Because we lose the grace of God that is in each of us for each of us. We lose the grace that comes horizontally. I believe in horizontal grace. It doesn't mean that I believe in grace while I'm sleeping, it means that I don't just believe the grace that comes through a crack in the ceiling, I believe the grace that comes through others of like faith who have the Holy Spirit of God.

John Calvin used to say of the church that God only dwells in the midst by dwelling in each one I tend to think of Him as in that central space or front space which is unoccupied, all of us clustering around Him, and that the grace is there in the empty space. It isn't! The grace is scattered through the whole community of believers. We too often imagine that God can only come to us through the ceiling, vertically, independent of any human being. But that isn't His only way of working. God's grace comes to us in a thousand ways. When we drift into a lonely and exclusive piety which insists on disembodied grace and private experience, we become starved and emaciated. We need the grace of God that is in each other. Others need the grace of God that is in us. That's why your church needs you. Never think your church doesn't need you because you're not prominent in ministry, talent or personality. You are like a piece of the jigsaw. Maybe you feel you're only a bit of the blue in the sky, seemingly commonplace. Nobody would miss me if I wasn't there! But take that very ordinary piece out of the jigsaw and what a gap there is in the whole picture – spoiled and incomplete because your shape is irregular and irreplaceable. Nobody can force any other shape into your space. No one else in your church is quite you. No one else can fill the place appointed by the Master for you. Your community needs you, your struggles and your victories, your experiences and your understanding.

'One anothering'

Biblical religion is social. We are called to community, not to isolation. We're not to be loners but brothers and sisters. We're not complete without others. We're not helped without others and we are not helpful without others. We can't be. And we cannot be holy alone. We are called to what John Stott long ago termed, 'one anothering'. We simply can't be private believers who don't bother with churches. Salvation is into the church, gifts are for the church, sanctification is within the church. That's why Paul writes to the Colossians: 'Let the word of Christ dwell in you richly as you teach and admonish one another with all wisdom, and as you sing psalms, hymns and spiritual songs with gratitude in your hearts to God.' No one is excluded from either the receiving or the giving of that grace. Everyone has something, no one has nothing. The church of Jesus Christ is a graced and gifted community. Grace and good things can come through the church, sometimes through some unlikely people in it – through the weak, not just through the strong.

Over my years in the church I've been privileged to serve, I've known some humble, troubled, and even difficult and awkward people, who came into their own at a crucial point. The church is not only for the well, but for the sick. The wounded person matters; we need them and they need us. If we're only interested in those whose presence flatters or profits us, then we grieve the Holy Spirit who treasures those we neglect. Human society and the church need their wounded, both to learn from and to care for: those who battle every day with physical disabilities and those who care for them; those who struggle with their sexuality and those who fall; those who have lost an easy faith, and found a hard one. In profound ways only the wounded can make us whole. Only they know some things, only they can teach us and complete us. We ourselves learn from our wounds. Our wounds may even prove to be our gifts.

Destroying the community

Just as God is in the business of creating community, so Satan is in the business of destroying community. That's why our unity as the people of God is so important. As evangelical people, we belong very much together, sharing a community of convictions on all the really big things. One of the most important things in our lives and for our effectiveness in the evangelisation of the world is that we recognise clearly our unity in the big things and handle wisely our diversity in

the secondary things. We do ourselves, as well as each other, a great
disservice when we are constantly suspicious of one another. We forget who our friends are and confuse them with our enemies. We have
a capacity for shooting ourselves in the foot In the sixties we fought
over Calvinism, and Arminianism, then it was separatism versus mixed
denominations; in the eighties it was the charismatic movement and
signs and wonders, and in the nineties it was women preaching and in
leadership. We keep doing it. I'm not advocating a church whose only
colour is battleship grey. We are a multicoloured people. Although I
sometimes wish everyone was like me, I'm rather glad they're not –
and so is my wife!

The involved community

Let me finally come from the community within to the wider community. We are not to be cut off from the community, but involved,
interacting with the community around us, and its various sub-
communities in the world – sport and politics, workplace life and
caring professions, schools and hospitals. In the Bible there is a worldliness which is forbidden and a worldliness that is commanded. This is
God's world, every inch of it, and we are called to reclaim it for God.
But we can only do so if the church is there for the healing of the
world. To do that, we ourselves must be in the process of being healed,
in our inner beings and our outer relationships. This is to be the testimony of the church in community – that God is repairing the world
and creating a new society which will inherit the earth because of
Jesus. As communities of people, united in faith and one in Christ and
the Spirit, we can startle the world. In our churches, our communities,
our community life and our relationships, we can be what the world
really wants to be but is constantly failing to be. Our world is fragmented and alienated. It's divided politically, economically, socially,
nationally, racially and linguistically; by temperament and personality,
talent and ability, and by contrary motivations and goals. A world falling
apart needs a people coming together. Our challenge in the churches
is this. We are to be caring communities in a world too preoccupied,

too defensive, to care; communities of love in a world very short on love. Communities which cherish and develop faith in a world which so often devalues and discourages or distorts it. To do all this, we have to be salt rubbed in – a people engaged in the workplace and the street, in local schools and councils, in politics and community care.

Accessible communities

As communities, we have to be welcoming as well as warning, accessible, not cut off. We have to build bridges of friendship that people can cross into communities of love because the longest distance in Britain is not between Land's End and John o'Groats, it's the distance between the safety of their homes and this strange alien territory called church. My experience has been that when they do come, they often detect an atmosphere of peace, love and good will, that we've come to take for granted, or perhaps believe is pretty low at this point in our church, but which to them is often something very striking and very welcome.

Our church, the Cornerstone Evangelical Church in Nottingham, isn't situated in one community. Most of our people come from all over the city and beyond. For the past ten years, because we outgrew our old buildings, we've rented a large school. It has very large halls and can accommodate us. It means all our money can go into missions instead of buildings which is wonderful for a start, but it's amazing how many people thought, how can you have church without a church? – by which they meant a building. How can you keep up the community life without a centre which is your own?

There are many ways of being and reaching the community. Recently, we had our own Cornerstone Jubilee Street Party with decorations, barbecue, live music and bouncy castle. Our musicians formed a scratch jazz band, and a large screen silently played the video of the Queen's fifty years in the great hall where everybody was eating. Hundreds came and brought their friends, for many of whom it was their first glimpse of a church – albeit a church at play, rather than worship. We did a similar thing on the millennium night where, after a wonderful evening of food and a presentation, on the stroke of mid-night we all welcomed in the new millennium, not with a cheer, but with the Lord's Prayer. Many visitors said they'd wanted to be part of something without the risk of drunkenness and trouble. They weren't Christians but they wanted to be part of something like this, and they were delighted and touched by a community which did things differ-ently. The difference wasn't alien because they met humanity and visitors bowed in prayer before the great realities at the borders of a new millennium.

For many years, people in our church have been involved in a soup run for the homeless and more recently, in the past year or two, a very strong work has grown up among the refugees, the asylum seekers, where many have come to know Jesus Christ as Saviour and Lord. Another work is done by some of our full time staff and many helpers for internationals, studying at the university and for their wives, who can be very lonely and cut off. This is a community doing what an individual could hardly do alone. I'm conscious that large churches often have large resources and can sometimes do a more high profile and dramatic work than most – and that we can be pushed and pres-sured into community work for which we may not be suited and made to feel guilty when we are simply being realistic. But small churches in small communities, too, can be lights in dark places which don't have to be big to be seen.

Where there's need there's usually Christians, and where there are churches they can be cities set on high places. Jesus' words, 'You are the light of the world' uses the plural you, and His picture of a city on a hilltop is a picture of communities of faith and love, not just soli-tary believers. We're all lights but we need to be altogether to be cities. To change the picture to one less familiar, we've all seen geese fly in that fascinating V formation. Do you know why they do it? Geese fly-ing in flock have 70 per cent greater range than a single goose on its own, because the downdraught of the bird in front gives uplift to the one behind. And geese in formation can fly 75 per cent faster than single geese because they fly against less wind resistance. We travel far-ther and faster together in the life of the kingdom, the communities of the Beatitudes; the communities of the King. Let's bow in prayer.

Submission to the King

by Victor Jack

VICTOR JACK

Victor became a Christian at the age of sixteen after a period of teenage rebellion. Two years in the army in Cyprus was a strengthening and maturing experience before moving on to Moorlands Bible College which prepared him for thirty-seven years of evangelism with Counties. Victor has served on the Board of Mission England, is currently Director of Sizewell Hall Conference Centre and an elder at his church. He worked as Chaplain at the Garden Tomb in Jerusalem for twelve years. Happily married to Meg, they enjoy their three sons as well as sports, hiking, gardening and travel.

Submission to the King
Mark chapter 8

Introduction

Have you ever received one of those exciting letters through the post that tell you that you have been personally selected in your community or your district to be awarded £50,000? But your enthusiasm begins to wane when you discover that there are other people in your community who have received a similar letter. And then as you read further down, you find in the small print that this wonderful gift isn't quite what it first appeared to be. You have to buy something in order to be entered for a prize draw. Or you have to pay £19.50 administration costs before you can be entered into the prize draw.

But when you come to the wonderful free offer that Jesus offers to us, of peace with God, of joy in the Holy Spirit and forgiveness through the Lord Jesus, you discover a completely different approach, one of honesty, openness and integrity. The honesty of Jesus stands out so clearly in Mark chapter 8 when He puts before us what it means to be one of His disciples. He tells us the truth, the whole truth and nothing but the truth. There's no small print in the contract, no hidden agenda. Jesus made no attempt to coerce people into His kingdom. He offered people then, as He does today, gifts that money cannot buy:

peace, joy, hope, freedom and a full and fulfilling life. But He also told them it would be challenging as well as fulfilling.

There have been some great leaders in history who have also been honest. In the early 1900s, Ernest Shackleton placed an advert in some of the London papers, inviting people to accompany him on his famous polar expedition. This is how he advertised for volunteers: 'Men wanted for hazardous journey. Small wages, bitter cold, long months in complete darkness. Constant danger. Safe return doubtful.' Sir Winston Churchill in the days of the Second World War said, 'All I can offer you is blood, sweat, toil and tears.' True men in their thousands answered the call, even though they knew full well what the cost involved would take from them.

The challenge to follow Christ

I wonder when you last heard an evangelistic message couched in the language that Jesus used when He was speaking not only to His disciples but also to the gathered crowd. He challenged them in these words: 'If anyone would come after Me, he must deny himself, take up his cross and follow Me. For whoever wants to save his life will lose it but whoever loses his life for Me and the gospel will save it.'

How big a response would we get if we advertised for Christian converts in this term? Don't you think that the Western Church has done something to Christianity that the early Christians wouldn't have believed was possible? We have made Christianity safe and comfortable. We've done a great disservice to the gospel message when we take out this challenging aspect of what it means to be a follower of Jesus. Could it be that this is the reason why some full-blooded men have not been attracted to the Christian faith? What we have presented is a diluted version of the call to arms that Jesus presents here.

Jesus made no attempt to lure men into His kingdom. He brought no pressure to bear. He even sent people away to think again: 'Count the cost,' He said. 'Look before you leap! Think through the challenge of what it's going to be if you're going to truly follow Me.' Jesus never lowered His standards. He asked the disciples in the first century and every would-be Christian since to give Him their full and total commitment. Nothing less will do.

I became a Christian in my middle teens. God demolished all the walls of pride and rebellion that I'd erected against Him. I offered my life to Jesus. But two or three years later I realised there were two sides to the coin in being a Christian. I had received from Jesus what He had offered. But had I really offered to Him what He was asking from me? He had laid down His life for me. Had I really made an unconditional surrender of my life to Him? I could take you to the old oak tree where I knelt and prayed and said, 'Lord forgive me. I've been living my Christian life just for what I could receive from You. I come now to offer my life back to You in all its fullness, for You to take and use in whatever way You choose.'

The call to follow Christ

The whole challenge of Christian discipleship comes to us through this passage in two ways. Notice in verse 34, Mark records 'He called the crowd to Him along with His disciples and said: "If anyone would come after Me ... "' Jesus was speaking to those who had started to follow Him, His own disciples, as well as those who were thinking about following Him. Those of us who are already Christians need constantly to be reminded of the kind of life that Jesus has called us to, the quality of discipleship that He expects and deserves. Those who are considering becoming Christians need to understand the depth of commitment that Jesus expects. To all of us Jesus says, 'If you would come after Me, then here are the conditions.' There are three that we need to look at.

Deny ourselves

'If anyone would come after Me, he must deny himself'. This simply means saying 'no' to my selfish, sinful desires and constantly saying 'yes' to the will of Christ in my life. The kind of self-denial that Jesus speaks of here has been terribly diluted to mean things like giving up chocolates or cigarettes for Lent. It's not just denying things to myself, but rather saying 'no' to every wrong desire that surges up from my corrupt sinful nature, every wrong attitude I'm inclined to adopt, every wrong action that I am about to take. Our lifestyles as Christians must be characterised by a daily discipline of saying 'no' to self and 'yes' to Christ. It will mean saying 'no' to my natural desire to be lazy and undisciplined. It will mean saying 'no' whenever I'm tempted to promote myself rather than Jesus. It will mean saying 'no' to those spiteful words that I don't need to say about another person. It will mean saying 'no' to sinful thoughts and actions. And it will mean saying 'yes' to Jesus in every situation.

The word for this is 'repentance' which is part of a genuine conversion to Jesus. It means an inward change of heart and mind that leads to a new change of direction. There may be wrong things in our lives that we feel we could never really be free from but if we're willing to repent and to renounce those things and cry to God for help, then He will bring it because Jesus promised: 'You will know the truth, and the truth will make you free.' No one can genuinely follow Jesus without this U-turn in their life where they forsake sin Every day I need to recognise the wrong desires and attitudes that surge up from this old nature that I have and be willing to say 'no'. Jesus put it in a very vivid way when He said, 'If your eye leads you into sin, pull it out. If your hand leads you into sin, cut it off.' But He didn't mean us to gouge out our eyes or to mutilate our bodies. It was a very vivid way of saying, we need to be ruthless with ourselves whenever we're tempted to do what we know is wrong before God and will grieve His Holy Spirit.

Take up your cross

Again this has been weakened to mean some sort of personal problem with my health, my family or job, so that with grim resignation we tend to say 'I suppose it's my cross and I will have to bear it.' But there's a far deeper meaning to these words than that of superficial interpretation: Jesus was calling His disciples to be ready for persecution, suffering and even death. It means we must if necessary be prepared to die for what we believe. Jesus is telling us that to follow Him, firstly, means that we must recognise that our old sinful nature needs to be nailed to the cross. Everything bad about us needs to be rejected and crucified.

Secondly, on becoming a Christian, we must be willing to accept the pain, shame and persecution that belonging to Jesus will surely bring in an evil and hostile world. Jesus said to His disciples as He sat on the hillside overlooking Galilee, 'Blessed are you when men insult you, persecute you, and falsely say all kinds of evil against you ...' He warned them of the kind of things that would happen if they followed Him faithfully. Paul reminds us in his letter, 'All those who live a godly life in Christ Jesus will be persecuted.' If we stand for what is true and right we will come into conflict with those who are doing what is evil and wrong. If we refuse to compromise our faith, we will in some way be persecuted; probably verbally, if not physically.

I was very challenged thinking about this as we've been working recently in Jerusalem. It made me realise that, in the west, we hardly know what it means to take up the cross for Jesus. We came across a Muslim man who had become a Christian. When he did, he had a wife and three children. But after he became a Christian, the father of his wife came and took his wife and three children away, and he has not seen them since. That's what it costs in some countries for people to stand by Jesus. We have to ask ourselves: why is it in countries where it costs so much to be a follower of Jesus that people are prepared to face that cost? Here where it costs comparatively little to be a Christian, we're not willing to stand for Jesus and the truth. We tend to compromise our faith so easily.

Jesus is asking that we willingly accept this rejection for His sake for He endured it for our sake. It was Dietrich Bonhoeffer who said 'When Christ calls a man, He bids him come and die' and there are, of course, different kinds of dying. Dying to self-centredness, selfish ambition, self-glorification, and in the end if necessary, being willing to die for Christ as a martyr. A missionary working in a dangerous situation in Africa was asked if she was afraid to die because of the hazardous conditions surrounding her. Her reply simply was, 'I died ten years ago.'

Lose our lives

What a challenging and thought-provoking paradox this is. If we try to save our lives we will lose them. But if we lose them to Christ and the work of His kingdom, we will find them. It simply means life lived and kept for self is life lost, empty and unfulfilled. But life given to Christ and the work of His kingdom is life found, fulfilled and kept for eternity. When we commit ourselves to Christ, we discover our true identity. We discover who we are: people made in the image of God. We find out how we should live for the glory of God and the blessing of others and we discover how we can die in the victory of Christ and with the assurance of heaven.

Jim Elliott was a young man that impacted the lives of many of us when I was younger. He was martyred in the jungles of Ecuador seeking to take the gospel to the Auca Indians. He wrote in his journal: 'He is no fool who gives what he cannot keep to gain what he cannot lose.' We cannot keep our lives, we can't hold on to them. We're programmed to die. But we can give our lives to gain what we cannot lose, the precious gift of eternal life and an inheritance in heaven for ever.

There's an inescapable paradox here that, for the most part, has been lost on our pleasure-seeking generation. Life has to be given in order to be discovered. You can only know if you have something worth living for when you discover it's worth dying for. Life must be spent, not hoarded. The world's attitude is, 'How much can I extract from life?' Our attitude if we're to be true followers of Jesus is simply, 'How much can I give to Christ and to others?' Life for a true disciple is given to us not to keep for ourselves but to give away to Jesus and to those around us. Here is the call to follow Christ, to deny ourselves, to crucify ourselves, and to lose ourselves to Christ and the work of His kingdom. Jesus isn't calling us to an easygoing kind of life, to the lukewarm commitment with which I began my Christian life. As an evangelist, in the later years of my ministry I have not talked to people about making a decision for Jesus but rather, 'Are you willing to make an unconditional surrender to Jesus Christ who laid down His life for you?' Nothing else is worthy of a response to Him.

Confess Christ

'If anyone is ashamed of me and my words in this adulterous and sinful generation, the Son of Man will be ashamed of him when He comes in His Father's glory with the holy angels' (verse 38). The decision to follow Jesus is a private, inward commitment, but it must be followed by an outward public confession of Christ. In these words Jesus is setting the scene of a public trial, which would become all too familiar to His listeners in a few years time. A Christian disciple would be standing before a pagan judge, not for any crime he'd committed against the government or the land, but simply because he is a Christian and the judge is giving him one last chance. 'Renounce this Jesus of yours and you can save your life and go home as a free man.' Jesus is saying, 'If you try to save your life by being ashamed of being identified with Me, then I will be ashamed of you.'

Isn't it incredible that we have the ability to make Jesus feel ashamed of us? But He's so intimately involved with us. You will know, if you have children, if they do well, you purr with pride but if they do badly, you can feel ashamed Jesus is saying, 'Whatever it costs you, don't be ashamed of Me. Whether at school or at work or at college or in the forces, stand for Me. If you don't, I will be ashamed of you.' And so the call is to confess Christ with our lips.

We must, as disciples of Jesus, be willing at every opportunity to speak for Him and to confess that we are one of His followers. 'Always be prepared,' Peter wrote in his letter, 'to give an answer to everyone who asks you for the reason of the hope within you. But be careful to always do it with gentleness and respect.' We must confess Christ with our lips and in baptism. This is an outward sign of our public allegiance to Him. We are nailing our colours to the mast, openly, unashamedly, admitting to friends, family and neighbours that we belong to Jesus and have brought our lives under His Lordship. This comes as a huge cost in some countries where if people are publicly baptised they can lose their jobs and their lives, and be imprisoned.

Then we must confess Christ with our daily lives. We're called to live a new quality of life and this is one of the passionate appeals that comes through so many of Paul's letters. 'Whatever happens, conduct yourselves in a manner worthy of the gospel of Christ.' People who are not Christians often set a higher standard for us than we set for ourselves. They know the kind of people that we ought to be. It was William Barclay who wrote, 'The only way to demonstrate their Christianity as the best of all religions is to show that it produces the best of all people.' Are we ashamed of Jesus? Do we feel so inhibited in some circles that we would never admit that we were one of His disciples? Have we forgotten that we are following the greatest teacher who ever lived, who left the finest example the world has ever seen, who made the greatest sacrifice the world has ever witnessed, and whose resurrection was the greatest miracle ever known? We can hold our heads high in any company.

The cost of following Christ

The call to follow and confess Christ is a huge challenge. It may be costly but there are three powerful motivations in this particular passage. The first is, we need to do this for our own sake. Many people have a deep seated fear that if they make this unconditional surrender of their lives to Jesus that somehow they will lose out. True, we may lose a few friends. We may have to say goodbye to some bad habits, but nothing can compare with the unspeakable privilege of knowing God as our Father, Jesus as our Saviour and the Holy Spirit as our Helper. To quote Paul, 'I consider everything a loss compared to the surpassing greatness of knowing Jesus Christ my Lord, for whose sake I have lost all things. I consider them as rubbish, that I may gain Christ'. Jesus simply asks us to give up the garbage in our lives so that He can replace it with the richness of His grace.

Profit and loss

To drive home this point, Jesus uses an illustration from the business world. 'What good is it for a man to gain the whole world, yet forfeit his soul? ... What can a man give in exchange for his soul?' Jesus placed – on a set of scales – the whole world on one side, and the individual person on the other. Then He asked a normal business-type question of profit and loss. Suppose you were to gain the whole world, and yet be lost from God? What kind of profit would you have made?

John Stott in *Basic Christianity* says, 'You would have made a very poor bargain for at least three reasons. For one thing, you cannot gain the whole world. For another, it would not last while you had it and thirdly, while it lasted it would not satisfy.'

What can a man give in exchange for himself? Of course it costs to be a Christian but it costs an awful lot more not to be. Everybody's racing after material things and yet they're like seawater; the more you drink of them, the more thirsty you become. The more you have the less you enjoy what you have got. Losing our souls is the equivalent of wasting our lives, missing the opportunity that God wants to give us to make our lives count for Him. We may gain success in the eyes of the world, but at the end we may have nothing to present to God. We brought nothing into the world and we can take nothing out, so what can anybody give in exchange for their soul? Nothing is valuable enough even to make an offer. Nothing can compensate for missing out on the precious gift of eternal life that Jesus offers. The thought of facing God's judgement and being excluded from His presence for ever is an appalling prospect when you take time to consider it seriously. So for our own sake we need to make this unconditional surrender of our lives to Jesus.

We also need to make it for the sake of others. Jesus spoke of losing our lives and then giving our lives for the sake of the gospel, so it's not just what we can receive but rather also what we can give. We're surrounded by people whose lives are broken, ensnared by powerful addictions, people whose hearts are breaking because of the pain in their family situations. How can we best help them? In practical ways of compassion, but primarily and supremely by sharing Jesus with them. There is no greater thrill than seeing the transforming power of the love of God at work in somebody's life.

The greatest motivation of all

But the real reason why we should make this offer of our lives to Jesus is for His sake. He said, 'Whoever loses his life for Me or for My sake will find it.' Here is the greatest motivation of all. We should be committed totally to Jesus, not just because of what we can receive, not just because of what we can give to others, but supremely because of what Jesus gave to us. How beautiful are those words: 'The Son of God loved me and gave Himself for me.' I'm convinced that only a fresh vision of Jesus impaled on a Roman cross bearing in His innocent person the guilt of our sin, will make us willing to deny ourselves, to crucify ourselves and to lose our lives in His. As C.T. Studd so eloquently expressed it, 'If Jesus Christ be God and gave Himself for me, then no sacrifice that I can make can ever be too great for Him.'

Becoming a Christian is a little bit like getting married. Both require great commitment. I often conduct a number of weddings each year, and as I stand before the young people making their promises, I often wonder if they realise what they're actually saying. But if the couple are to know the joys and the rewards of marriage, then that commitment must be made and maintained day after day. The same is true in our relationship with Jesus. The reward is great. He offers us life as it was meant to be lived, but there is a cost as we say to Jesus: 'For better or worse, Jesus, for richer or poorer, Jesus, in sickness and in health, Jesus. But praise God, death will never separate us.' Hear Jesus saying: 'This is My body, given for you.' How do we respond? There is only one fitting response – 'Lord Jesus, here is my body, given for You.'

Children of the King

by Dominic Smart

DOMINIC SMART

Minister in Dundee for ten years, Dominic moved back to Aberdeen three years ago, his wife's home town and where he had spent his study years, to be Minister of Gilcomston South Church. Gilcomston is a thriving city-centre church in Europe's oil capital, with a long tradition of expository teaching and an increasing engagement in city-centre witness and ministry. As well as speaking at conferences and universities, Dominic teaches on Christian communication at the Highland Theological College. With four children, two rabbits, two cats and a dog, his hobby is trying to catch up on sleep!

Children of the King
Galatians 4:1 – 7

Our theme is holiness, living as children of the King. I find it extremely interesting and encouraging that when the convention committee were thinking about this theme, they chose this passage. Normally when we are thinking of holiness, we're thinking about not sinning. We define sins in certainly a biblical way – those things that we do which are displeasing to God – but what we usually think of are what we might call the sins of the flesh. Paul writes about that in Galatians (5:19-21) but Galatians is really about a different kind of sin. It is not a sin by which we indulge the flesh, it is that sin by which we place confidence in the flesh. That's the phrase Paul used to describe himself in his Judaistic days before he came to Christ. He placed his confidence in the flesh. It is the religious sin of legalism. It encourages me that the convention committee had the sensitivity to where many of us are in our own lives, so instead of being asked to tell us all not to have wrong sexual relations with people, not to go betting, gambling, getting drunk and all the rest of it, I should be asked to preach from the word of God about this problem that we face in our lives and in our fellowships, that is so characteristic of our evangelicalism in the west nowadays.

Legalism

It is the sin in the Scriptures of going back to Judaism or of going and learning it for the first time. It was sown within so many of the churches that Paul had planted, by the Judaisers, who came most likely from Jerusalem, following Paul around to undo the work that he had been doing, as he preached the gospel of grace. What the Judaisers taught was that if you wanted to enjoy the covenant of God's blessings, then you had first of all to put yourself in a position to receive those by your works. You had to qualify for Christ, in effect. If you wanted to enjoy the blessings of the new covenant in Jesus Christ, to pick up on the language of Hebrews in the New Testament and Jeremiah in the Old Testament, then you had to observe the ordinances of the old covenant. That was the preaching and the teaching of the Judaisers. They dogged the growth of the church as Paul planted churches all around the Mediterranean. It was a huge problem.

The heart of legalism…

We need to define it carefully because all of us have a knee-jerk reaction against legalism. We all would run a million miles from it, we wouldn't want it, so we say, and yet we find ourselves enmeshed by it, very often, in our fellowships. But we need to be careful to define just what legalism is all about if we take it out of that strict context of – well, it was particularly circumcision in Galatians chapter 6. What was the core of the message that the Judaisers were bringing to these churches and by which they were confusing these young Christians?

It was that you lead a life which seeks acceptance with God by the keeping of rules and regulations and seeks to maintain that acceptability with God by the keeping of rules and regulations. We have rules in our fellowships and that is good, we need them. We need order. God has built laws into life generally so that it goes well. The opposite to legalism is not lawlessness. Lawlessness in the Scriptures is never a good thing. It is no more than anarchy and pride. Christian freedom is not freedom to do what we want. Not one of us down here is fit to be let loose with that. There will come a day when we are, but we won't be down here then, we'll be in glory.

... and its opposite

The opposite to legalism is resting in the acceptance that we have with God in Jesus Christ. The opposite to legalism is not 'no laws': the opposite to legalism is grace. If you go to the kind of fellowship where most folk would get dressed up on Sunday and you don't want to – don't think that's necessarily a legalistic fellowship. You can go to a fellowship where nobody gets dressed up on Sunday morning and some would find that almost as legalistic. The opposite to legalism is not the absence of rules spoken or unspoken; the opposite of legalism is grace. There's living with God and therefore with one another, according to the acceptance we have in Christ, from the first moment of our spiritual lives, right the way through to glory.

The attraction of legalism

Notice first of all that legalism is a very big problem in the New Testament. It is a constant problem that Paul faces, as he writes to and visits churches, as he receives reports of how fellowships were getting on. It is a problem, now as then, for those who are keen about leading a holy life. We want to protect ourselves from sin so we can very readily hedge our lives around with all sorts of rules and regulations in order not to sin. It's a good motivation which leads to a legalistic view of life. It was a good motivation that lay behind the scribes, the teachers of the law, it was a good motivation that lay even behind the Pharisees – they wanted not to sin.

Legalism is a big problem, then as now, for those who are insecure. Some of us love rules and regulations. Temperamentally we are disposed to that kind of thing. Maybe we've got some insecurities and we feel more comfortable if there are lots of rules. Some parents are like that with their children – something goes tragically wrong, there'll be five new rules in the house before the kids get to bed.

Some people find rules very comforting as young Christians, and young Christians can be very susceptible to those in fellowships who like to impose rules upon them. It's a big problem, then as now, for young Christians. There's also a big problem for us in our pride because we think that we can make ourselves acceptable to God. We keep the rules, we're doing fine, God must therefore love us; that is — we are strong when we are strong. We are acceptable to God when we are doing well, not when Jesus did perfectly well for us. It's a specially plausible problem, then as now, because it just seems so right that we should have lots of rules. After all, God gave ten, and there was no immediate verse in the Old Testament that could be pointed at to say that those ten would be thrown away as Paul seemed to be teaching.

Paul on legalism

Paul reserves some of his biggest guns for the problem of legalism. He calls the Judaisers and those who were listening to them, first of all, hypocrites (Gal. 2:13). They're actors, they're putting on a performance; there's nothing genuine in their spirituality and their relationship with God, it's just an act. They're agitators (5:12), they're stirring things up, in a fellowship that should know the peace of God. They are causing storms, left, right and centre. They are eternally condemned (1:8), fairly strong language. They have a penalty to pay (5:10) and then Paul says something that you would never open your women's rural meeting with; it's the most astonishing piece of bluntness (5:12), 'As for those agitators, I wish they would go the whole way and emasculate themselves!' He reserves very strong language for the problem of legalism.

How does he help these Galatians to get out of the mess that they've got themselves into with it? The logic of Galatians is that he does so by drawing sets of contrasts between the two ways to live before God and he does so in these terms: you can live by the gospel that I preached (1:11) or the different gospel that is really no gospel at all (1:6-7). You can live by faith (2:16) or you can live by trying to observe the law (3:10 onwards). You can live according to the promise that God has given (3:16), the covenant with Abraham, or you can try to live according to the law. You can live according to the line of Sarah (4:21 onwards), or you can try to live according to the law – a kind of Sinai Christianity, according to the old covenant and not according to the new covenant with Abraham that has been fulfilled in Christ or that covenant. You can be one who lives according to the line of Sarah (4:21 onwards) or you can live according to the line of Hagar, the law line, the legalist line – interesting to note there that Hagar was always meant to be Sarah's maidservant.

The law was always meant to serve the people of God, and not the other way round. You can live according to freedom (5:4) or you can live according to slavery. You can live according to the Spirit (5:16) or according to the sinful nature. Same kind of contrast in chapter 3:1-5. He sets up these contrasts and he has one here (4:1-7). He says, 'You can live the way you were before you were redeemed or you can live the way that you actually have become in Christ *de facto* – whether you feel it or not or think it or not – after you were redeemed.' He sets up this before and after. He's saying, 'Don't go back to what you were before. What you were before has gone.' He's setting up a contrast; before you were redeemed; after you were redeemed.

Before and after

The curse of the law

We need to look at what made the difference between those two and then we need to refocus on what Paul is so concerned about in this passage. He writes – before you were redeemed – you were under the curse of the law (3:10-13). Break one, you've broken them all. You're not justified by trying to keep the law; you're going to end up condemned by the very law which you are trying to use as a ladder to lead you up to God. The rungs will not bear your weight, the weight of your sinfulness is too strong for them, and you will find that it's been leaning up against the wrong wall all the time anyway.

He's writing about being under the governance of the law (4:4,5). The vocabulary is very interesting. If we were to go back just a few verses, we would see the first word that he uses (3:23,24). 'Before this faith came, we were held prisoners by the law'. What it meant to be under the governance of the law was that you were imprisoned, shut up on all sides. It's the word that is used in fishing, for being caught in a net – you were enmeshed by this, struggle as you could you would never escape but only get yourself further entangled. Chapter 3 verse 24, you were under the charge of what in the Authorised Version is termed a schoolmaster to lead us to God. 'Schoolmaster' is not really the most helpful translation for us of the word. The word is *paedagogos* and was a reference to a slave who would work in a free family's house – who wouldn't actually be a teacher but would take the children to the schoolteacher's house.

Chapter 4 verse 2 – the word is guardian, *epitropos*. Paul is pulling on all his vocabulary to emphasise what it means to be under the governance of the law. The *epitropos* would have responsibility in charge of the children within the house, would lead them by example, watch out for them, protect them, but who would never be allowed to let them out of his sight. The child would never be allowed to do anything without the permission of the *epitropos*. Then the fourth word – trustees, superintendents. There are some Christian circles, churches, and church organisations and other Christian organisations that talk about superintendents and wardens.

Paul piles these words on top of each other; you were imprisoned, you had a guardian and a guide, you had this *epitropos* over you, without whose permission you wouldn't dare breathe, you had superintendents watching over you. To be a young child amounted to be a slave. You were in bondage, you had no rights, yoked to the person who was put in charge over you, the guardian. You might end up owning everything in future years at a time when your father thought you were fit to handle it, but under these governors, you were powerless.

We have a little boy, two years old, Matthew. Matthew may well inherit one day all those vast riches which I have to pass on to him – but at the moment he has no rights at all. He only receives what we give him, other than what he nicks out of the cupboard for himself. For the child, who is no different to a slave (verse 1); although he owns the whole estate, everything that the father has for him, the

whole estate is just a matter of potential. It's off there in the future. All
he can do is wait, he cannot enjoy it. The best biblical picture to convey that to us is actually the children of Israel before they got into the
Promised Land. It was just all promised.

And after…

Now, says Paul, consider what you were like after you were redeemed.
Consider the difference. Everything that the Lord taught you to wait
for, that the whole Old Testament pointed to, now is yours in Jesus
Christ. He pursues the imagery that he has been using thus far.
Having said 'But' at the beginning of verse 4, he says 'Now you have
received the full rights of sons.'

If you've got the New Revised Standard Version I think that you've
got not 'sons' there in verse 5, but one of the most unhelpful bits of
politically correct paraphrasing that could ever have been put into a
Bible. You've got 'children' which defeats the whole contrast between
'before' and 'after', because you were children before and you're children after; it doesn't work. It means 'sons' because it was the sons who
did the inheriting in those days, the girls didn't.

He says, 'Now you have received the full rights of sons, you have
received everything that the Father has for you. You are fully grown
up in Christ,' to pursue the imagery, 'you have come of age, you are
no longer under the law. You are freed from those restrictions, from
that enmeshment and imprisonment, which was the law as a means of
trying to earn your rightness with God; you have been freed from
everything that effectively disinherited you. You have come of age and
are free to live directly with your Father, to speak to Him in a new
way. Now you can move around at His will, take responsibility for the
way the estate goes. Everything that you were waiting for now is
yours. Everything that you could never reach because the ladder
would never be tall enough and you'd always be falling off that law
ladder; everything that you were reaching for is given to you.

The Spirit of sonship

The second way in which he describes 'after' is: 'You have received the
Spirit of sonship whereby you cry "Abba, Father, Daddy".' It's a

curious word, is Abba. It is intimacy. We are right to think that it means 'Dad'. But it is also a term of respect. In calling Him Dad, it is never a term of mere familiarity. It is never glib, never facile, it would never just trip off the tongue as if it meant nothing. It has about it the most profound respect and intimacy; it has love about it. It is the cry that comes from one who knows that in a crowded supermarket, that word, with that voice, will be heard by one person who will respond. We have received the Spirit who cries out, Abba! That intimacy of relationship; no slave would ever dream of saying that.

The inheritance

The third thing, he says, that you are after you're redeemed, 'You are those who have received an inheritance.' You have received the inheritance of all the covenant blessings that God promised to Abraham. It's the word, the heirs, that goes back to verse 29 of chapter 3. If you belong to Christ then you're Abraham's seed and heirs according to promise; heirs of everything that God promised to Abraham. You're heirs of the promise that says, 'I will be your God', and 'You will be My people.' As Paul impresses upon them not to go back to being like slaves, what has made the difference? What has been the hinge by which this great turn has been made? It has been the work of Jesus Christ.

The time has come

Notice how Paul describes Christ's work in verses 4 and 5: 'But when the time had fully come' that is, when the Father had judged that it was precisely the right time, and the right time means not only that circumstances were fortuitous for spreading the gospel but the right time also contains that moment when the opposition to Christ would be not only intense from the Pharisees, but politically connected within the Sanhedrin and to the Roman authorities so that the crucifixion could actually happen in the way that it did. The time being right was a reference not only to things being fortuitous and good for the spread of the gospel, but for the hostility to have reached a particular point that would be focused upon Christ.

'But when the time had fully come, God sent his Son, born of a woman, born under law, to redeem those under law.' He sent his Son from heaven to become one of us, born under the governance of the law so that we in Him might become sons who then have all the inheritance. There is the reference to the cross that we notice in the term 'redeem' because redemption was accomplished at a price. Notice that Paul is also talking about the incarnation. He came down to become one of us, so that we in Him, in the Son, might become also sons. He came down, He who has all the inheritance of heaven and earth, as one of us, so that we, united with Him in His humanity, might become also those with an inheritance. It is by union with Christ in His death and resurrection that we are redeemed from under the governance, the entrapment, of the law. The cross is the lowest point of a path that started at the highest point, came down and it was at that lowest point that we were totally picked up, so that we also then might be raised to share because there will be a glory that will not only be revealed to us but revealed in us (Rom. 8:18 onwards).

What is at stake here?

Paul reasons with these people. He uses the kind of lifestyle that they would have been used to, to try and get them out of this big problem. What is at stake here? One the emotional, psychological and spiritual well-being of the children of God. What they have if they go back to that Judaism is an enslaved life all over again (4:8-11). They have a joyless life (4:15).

Our legalistic fellowships are the most joyless places on earth. Particularly, we would note, it is joylessness with respect to receiving the word of God (4:25). The word of God does not bring us joy, receiving the word of God just burdens us even more. Another thrashing from the minister! Or a beating up from the elders or another look from that guy over in the church that just tells me I've failed again … It is a burdened life (5:1). It just weighs you down. It's a futile life because you'll never keep it up.

What's at stake is the emotional, psychological, spiritual well-being of God's children and that's very important to God. It's not simply that Paul is pandering to twenty-first century self-indulgent Christians, it is important to God that we know His joy and receive His word with joy and know His freedom that has been purchased at such cost.

The witness that was carried to the watching world

A miserable life is a false life and it's no witness. It's as if you're taking the law that has been written in your heart and you're writing it back on external stuff and trying to press it on people from the outside. It's a miserable life. It's a non-gospel, it's bad news that we take to people, if we model with our living and talk in our churches in a way that says that the gospel is living this kind of legalistic life, then we just give people bad news, it's not good news.

Most of all what is at stake here is the worship of God and the glory that is due to His name. That's the biggest tragedy, when our fellowships are infected by endemic legalism. The worship of God and the glory that is due to His name just goes. You see, we get the glory for doing well at our rule-keeping. We don't feel glorious, we feel yet more miserable for not keeping them very well, but we are keeping some, so we do get some glory that should go to God. If the Redeemer gets no glory for such a costly redemption, the Father is no longer the Father of mercies and the God of all comfort, the Spirit is no longer our guide. Grace is no longer grace, mercy is no longer mercy. We do not worship God and give God the glory due to His name from those who have received the full rights of children of God who have come of age in Christ. It's one of the biggest problems in the New Testament. It was what was knocking more Christians out of the saddle than naughty living. If it wasn't for that problem of legalism we wouldn't have Galatians, we wouldn't have bits of Colossians, we wouldn't have bits of Philippians, we wouldn't have all those exchanges between Christ and the Pharisees, who taught the traditions of men and preferred them over the word of God. I am just so thankful that we have had even these few minutes to come to a God who treats us with such mercy, and who elevates His children not by making them feel wonderful about themselves, but by causing them to see the wonders of His grace and His mercy and His glorious redemption. Amen.

The King is among us

by Rico Tice

RICO TICE

Born in Chile, the son of a businessman and a nurse, Rico grew up in Uganda and Zaire. He studied History at Bristol University where he captained the rugby side. His progress towards full time Christian ministry began with a period as Lay Assistant at Christ Church, Clifton, before training for ordination at Wycliffe College, Oxford. He joined the ministry team at All Souls Church, Langham Place, in 1994 and has spent the last seven years developing the *Christianity Explored* course which is being used countrywide by churches and student groups.

The King is among us
John 16:5 – 16

As we look at the work of the Holy Spirit under the title: 'The King is among us' we'll find that the Christian wonderfully has been joined by an expert, the Spirit of Christ. Not only is His presence with you wherever you go essential to you but this passage will even tell us why it's a good thing that Jesus is no longer around. Actually it's obvious that it's a good thing that Jesus is not with us now in a human body and therefore limited to one geographical location. If He was, you would have as much chance of being with Him in your lifetime as you would a holiday with the Queen. You might get a five minute slot in His diary in 2030 or something but as it is, Christ the King is with me and in me by His Spirit every minute of every day wherever I go.

We're never alone

If we can flick back now, to Jesus' promise to the disciples in John 14:16-18. 'I will ask the Father, and He will give you another Counsellor to be with you for ever – the Spirit of truth. The Bible makes it clear that the Christian life is not just about a Creator God Who is up there and it's not just about looking back to the figure of Jesus two thousand years ago. The essence of the Christian life is not distance but presence, the close personal indwelling presence of the Holy Spirit in my life now, who draws me to Christ. I'm never alone. Speaking as a single person, that is so precious. As I see how fleeting my life is, I know that I'm never alone – Christ is with me, and I am rooted in eternity because of Him. That was a huge reason that I became a Christian. When my godfather was killed on the 6th August 1983, no one in my family had an answer to his death. Death severs loving relationships and I felt a terrible cosmic loneliness. I never feel that now because the Spirit of the Lord Jesus Christ is with me.

Two weeks ago I visited Anne Kneller, a member of the church family, in hospital. She is eighty-eight and she's terribly sick. When I arrived in the ward to see her, the sight of her just stopped me in my tracks; her face was slumped into an oxygen mask and her eyes were shut. I later found that she could not move her arms. I woke her and she said, 'Rico, the doctor tells me that no part of my body is working properly.' But then she said to me with total sincerity, 'But the Lord is so good, Rico.' She recited Ephesians 1:3 to me, and she meant it with all her heart. She knew the presence of the Lord Jesus by his Spirit. I walked out of the hospital and I was so moved I just burst into tears. I said to the Lord, 'Please help me to die like that, with that sense of Your sovereignty and Your presence.' I'm so grateful to Anne for that model of how to die well. Such talk of death brings us right into the middle of this teaching on the Holy Spirit in John's gospel.

The promise of another Comforter

Within the hour, Jesus would be betrayed. Within twenty-four hours he would be crucified, judicially murdered. Jesus is addressing His disciples in the upper room, on the threshold of these events. Imagine the pathos of the scene. It's a terrible thing to be told a loved one will die. It doesn't really get any worse because love is so hard to come by. It's not surprising Jesus says, 'Because I have said these things, you are filled with grief' (Jn. 16:6). They love this man! Since chapter 13, Jesus has been seeking to prepare the disciples for the tragedy that will engulf them. He's predicted that He will be betrayed by Judas and even denied by Peter, and they will all run away when He faces the test of His arrest and trial. But He has comforted them in chapter 14. They're going to desert Him; He comforts them. That's Jesus.

In chapter 14, He comforts them with the promise of another comforter, the same as Jesus, Who will strengthen and help them. He's taught them that although they will not see Him any more in His earthly body, yet their connection with Him will be as real as the connection of the branches into the stem of the vine. 'You will not be alone.' You are not alone. They, as the disciples of the Lord Jesus, need to remain in Him (Jn. 15:5), to keep asking Him for all they need, being utterly dependent; loving one another and obeying His commandments.

The world will hate you

That is especially important because Jesus teaches them in chapter 15 that the world is going to hate them. Have you come to terms with that yet? Three things the world hates about Jesus: His unique claims, His high and holy standards, and His free offer of salvation. It hates Christ, His purity and it wants to earn salvation on merit. In such a world, the disciples are not only to keep going but they must also testify to Christ (15:27). That's also to us. The root word 'testify' would have sent a shiver down their spines because it's the same root at the verb to be martyred. To testify has a cost. I remember when I was at theological college, Enoch Tombe, from the Sudan where tens of thousands of Christians have been martyred, said as he left in 1994, 'I'm going back to die with my people.' The command verse 27 is followed by the warning of 16 verse 2: 'They will put you out of the synagogue; in fact, a time is coming when anyone who kills you will think he is offering a service to God.'

It's taking up that theme of the requirement of the church in every generation to testify to the Lord Jesus, whatever that may cost, that leads us into these verses here. We learn why the Holy Spirit has been given and what He does both in the world and in the church. I want to focus on His work in the world (verses 8-11). For an evangelist seeking to prepare God's people for works of service (Eph. 4:11-12), it is crucial that the church family I serve see how the Holy Spirit is the lynchpin in our efforts to testify to Christ in a hostile world. We must get this teaching clear. He doesn't just leave us with a load of tips or techniques. He leaves us with a person who is far more powerful than any situation we may find ourselves in. We'll see in these verses that the work of salvation from beginning to end is the work of God. We do have our part to play but ultimately this work is dependent on the Spirit of Christ's transcendent power. It is God's power that turns lives around.

The Holy Spirit's work

The word 'convict' here is drawn from the law courts. It's the word used in the Greek-speaking world for cross-examination in the dock. The Holy Spirit comes to cross-examine people. He is the Spirit of truth with a capital T (verse 13) and so He presses home to people the truth about their lives. He shows them what they are really like. He's not after a 'guilty' verdict, that is already there – rather He's concerned that they see their desperate state before God and their need of mercy.

Recently I was coming out of Tesco's with my shopping and it suddenly poured. I immediately shouted: 'Taxi!' When I came out of Tesco's, I saw no need of a taxi but when the rain came, it made me see my need of rescue. That's a pathetic illustration of the Spirit's work in the world. A person who may have lived their whole life careless and indifferent to God can suddenly be arrested by a sense of sin. If you come from a non-Christian family and you bury people who die without Christ, that is a wonderful truth, to know that He can do that work, of showing them their sin. This is why I don't give up hope that loved ones, friends and colleagues, will become Christians. For the Holy Spirit makes the non-Christian sees their need of salvation. It may be a very sudden thing, it may be gradual, but He will be convicting them of guilt. Don't give up hope, because if He did the miracle of convicting me, He can definitely do it for them. I've just got to keep saying my prayers for them to be convicted of sin. How are your prayers going? It's so hard to keep going, isn't it? It's a real battle to say our prayers.

Sin is deeper

The Spirit convicts people that sin is deeper than they ever thought. People who once saw sin as someone else's problem, as naughty but nice, as just a sort of religious word about lust and laziness, suddenly see that sin is far more penetrating than that. They stop saying, 'If you knew my circumstances you'd understand why I have to do this.' Most strikingly of all, they begin to see that the essence of sin is a declaration of independence against God. Sin is saying, with Adam and Eve in the Garden, 'It may be your world, God, but I will run my life my way. I'll decide what good and evil is, what morality is.'

As the Holy Spirit opens people's eyes He begins to testify about Jesus (15:26), so Jesus gets bigger and bigger and bigger. They see that they have treated Him with total contempt. Jesus has been utterly ignored and therefore the ultimate yardstick of sin comes in verse 9: 'Because men do not believe in me'. This is the ultimate yardstick of sin, that people refuse to believe in God's Son. They reject Christ as God and therefore Lord of their lives.

Furthermore they refuse even to believe in His rescue. He paid in death and blood so that people might have eternal life and to reject Jesus is not an intellectual exercise, it is a sin. It is the very heart of sin and when the Spirit begins to work in a person's life, He shows them that sin. They see that they've been wrong about Jesus, and that their unbelief in Him is going to be their undoing. Can we begin to see what it therefore means here to keep in step with the Spirit, as J.I. Packer says, quoting from Galatians 5:25: 'What does it mean, according to this verse, for you and I to keep in step with the Spirit?'

Who are the most evil people?

How did you feel when you saw that Dr Harold Shipman had murdered at least 215 people? Did you not feel rage at that evil? As we hold on to that rage we felt, let's look at verse 9. Who, according to the Spirit, are the most evil people in history? It's your charming relation or colleague who refuses to believe in Jesus. That is the heart of human sin – rejection of Jesus. It is that that ultimately damns the world. If we really cared about loving Jesus, as the Spirit does, if we were really on the Spirit's wavelength, then we would be horrified that people refuse to believe in Jesus, that they suppress the truth by their wickedness (Rom. 1:18). How serious do we think this is? The Spirit reveals to people it is the essence of sin.

Ben and Annie work in the café next door to me. I live in a basement flat and they feed me all the time, I always go to that café. They are delightful and this is the issue. They hold Jesus at arm's length; they refuse to believe in him. I have great affection for them. It means they are operating right at the heart of human evil, if I'm to think biblically. It's no small thing to refuse to believe in Jesus. Can I remind you that in Romans 9 Paul wept about His people that they didn't believe in Jesus. I challenge you – when did you last weep about this? I come from a non-Christian home, it's easy for me to weep about the lost. I sometimes think that people who have the privilege of a Christian home don't realise how desperate it is that people turn their back on Jesus.

Righteousness is higher

The Spirit will also convict people in regard to righteousness (verse 10). No one can bluff it with Jesus, so a Samaritan woman is told (Jn. 4:17) when she tries to bluff over her relationships with men. Do you remember what He says to her? 'You are right when you say you have no husband. The fact is, you have had five husbands, and the man you now have is not your husband.' In chapter 8, Jesus sent a bunch of religious hypocrites away from a stoning to survey their own consciences with the words: 'If any one of you is without sin, let him be the first to throw a stone.' When Jesus was around there was no problem persuading people that God's righteousness was higher than they ever thought or could reach. People went through the experience of Peter in Luke 5, who shouted, 'Get away from me, Lord, I'm a sinful man!' That was the presence of Jesus, wonderfully loving and warm but also righteousness. But what do you do about convincing people of the absolute and inescapable moral claim of God when Jesus has gone to the Father? What happens then when people try bluffing God by saying: 'Righteousness is really a case of scraping by with 50 per cent from a soft judge, just do your best!' What do the disciples do then, when Jesus has suddenly gone? How do you persuade people that righteousness is beyond them then?

The work of the Spirit

He will press home to people's consciousness the righteousness of God. He'll cause the unbeliever to see that Jesus is the only way by which sinners like us can ever be made right with a holy God. You can be wandering through life and suddenly see that you can't do it when all along you thought you could. You get people saying, 'I've been good enough! I don't steal. I keep the Ten Commandments. I give to charity. I'm a good enough person for God. He's lucky to have me around. I've not been a murderer or a rapist, I've not done anything evil like that!' One person on *Christianity Explored* said to me four years ago, 'I give blood!' That what was going to put him right before God! Others don't go for moral reasons; they say, 'I go to church. I'm an Anglican. I've been baptised, I've been confirmed, I pray, I read the Bible, I go to communion, and because of all those reasons, I'm good enough!' But when the Spirit of Jesus does His work and teaches us about righteousness, people say: 'None of this will do me any good.' They see the sin of their own heart. They see that 'I cannot be right before God because I'm moral or religious. The Holy Spirit reveals to me that my sin is so great that all I can do is trust in what the Lord Jesus has done and receive that gift.'

What is the great work that He needs to do in my friends and yours? He has to persuade people that they are not good people going to heaven, which is what they think, but sinners going to hell. They will flee to the cross as the Spirit causes them to see that Christ's righteousness alone is what they must depend on. The mark of the authentic Christian is therefore constant awareness of our sin, and a constant gratitude for the righteousness of Christ that has been won for us on the cross. That is why thanksgiving is crucial to the Christian life. It's absolutely essential that every day I'm giving thanks for Christ's gift of righteousness because of my own sin, which I see every day in my Bible reading. How is your thanksgiving going?

Three years ago I was having a hard time, and I saw John Chapman, this Aussie clergyman. He said to me, 'Rico, it is obvious to me that there is no thanksgiving in your life. Every morning and every night, I want you to kneel by your bed and give thanks to God. Just list the good things.' That one thing has changed my life and my heart. Are you giving thanks?

Judgement is closer

Christ's Holy Spirit is able to convince the non-Christian world that sin is deeper, righteousness is higher, and lastly judgement is closer than they ever imagined (verse 11). Satan here is called the prince of this world because the world largely follows his delusions by rejecting Christ. He and the world which follows him face judgement. The person who is under the conviction of the Spirit will realise that judgement is not something like cancer – which may happen, and if it does, I'll face it then – the person under conviction realises the wrath of God is hanging over them, His settled, controlled, personal hostility to all that is wicked and sinful. They'll see that judgement is for real, because the Holy Spirit has done his work. In evangelism today people say, 'Don't talk to people about the future, they're not interested!' No, they're not interested until the Spirit does His convicting work. Then their blind eyes are opened. If people say, 'Just talk about this life when you talk about evangelism,' they're denying the fact the Spirit does open people's eyes to the future.

The Holy Spirit injects an imperative call for decision into our consciences. We see that in the Bible God's judgement is not set against God's goodness. It's proof of His goodness. He will not co-exist with evil. I can rest easy about Harold Shipman, about this dreadful thing that he has done, because God will bring him to judgement. Hebrews 4:13 is true: 'Nothing in all creation is hidden from God's sight. Everything is uncovered and laid bare before the eyes of Him to Whom we must give account.' How is the unbeliever ever to come to terms with this disastrous thought of their condemnation? The Spirit will persuade them that one day they will stand before a righteous God, and I've just got to preach that, teach that. Lovingly, with tears, say it.

Only the Spirit is able to convince the non-Christian world that sin is deeper, righteousness is higher, and judgement is closer than ever they had imagined. He does that work.

What is my job?

Amid all this work of the Spirit, this miraculous work of conviction and conversion, what is my job? 'You also must testify' (Jn. 15:27). To speak with tears of these great truths, and to trust that as I do that, the Spirit will do his convicting work in the world. To know that as I speak to someone of sin and judgement and its seriousness, that I have an ally in their hearts, the Holy Spirit of God doing battle with their conscience, nagging at them, pulling at them, convicting them, saying inside, this is true, this is true, even though everything in your relativistic education tells you it's not true, it's true. We just have to speak and teach it and the Spirit will do His work. The terrible tragedy is that we've stopped believing the Holy Spirit can do this convicting work. We have dishonoured him terribly. We aren't telling people with tears and love that the gospel is about being saved from hell, through the cross, for heaven. We're changing that because we're embarrassed by it. We're not saying it's about Christ who saves me from the wrath to come. As we change the gospel we show that we don't believe the Holy Spirit can do His work, which is a terrible blasphemy and we show that we don't love people enough to tell them the truth. If I warn people, I am the loving one. But we have got it into our heads that to not warn them is the loving thing to do. Our culture is sick of spin. It does actually want people to be straight with them.

This truth came home to me so forcibly when I was at Oxford. I was playing rugby for the university when I was at theological college, and there was a bloke there called Dave, and we became good friends. There was another guy in the rugby club called Ed, and I gave him a tape of a sermon I'd preached on John 1 verse 29, 'Behold, the Lamb of God, who takes away the sin of the world!' In that sermon I said simply, 'Either you can pay for your sin yourself in hell, or you can allow the Lamb of God to pay for you.' One evening after supper, for a bit of a laugh, Ed got the tape out and they listened to it together, four non-Christians. Dave was there. He was absolutely livid as he heard it. Afterwards he said, 'Rico is not my friend.' They said, 'Of course he is!' He said, 'If he was my friend, he would have warned me. If he really believes this, he'd have warned me.' Ed, a non-Christian, had to ring me up to tell me, 'He's very upset you've not said anything about this before.' The Spirit had done His work but I had not done mine.

Can I ask you three questions? Do you believe the Spirit will do His work in John 16 verses 8 to 11? He's done it in you, do you believe He can do that? Secondly, do you love people? Who do you therefore need to warn? We all have to do it. If we believe this and love people, we will warn people.

Submission to the King

by Peter Maiden

PETER MAIDEN

Keswick's current Chairman and Associate International Director of Operation Mobilisation, Peter is a very busy man! He travels extensively to fulfil his commitment with OM – overseeing the day-to-day co-ordination of its ministries in eighty-two countries. Peter is also an elder at Hebron Evangelical Church in Carlisle, where he lives, and manages to fit itinerant Bible teaching in the UK and overseas into his schedule. Peter enjoys family life with his wife Win and their three children and grandchild, as well as endurance sports. In particular he loves fell walking and long distance running and cycling.

Submission to the King
2 Timothy 2:8 – 13

We've certainly had a great week this week, God has spoken very clearly to us. But now for home and a very different context in which to live the Christian life. You probably won't be surrounded by Christians most hours of the day. You won't have the experience of singing the praise of God with thousands of others next Sunday. You might be struggling to find an organist rather than enjoying this brilliant band. We could continue with the contrast between our Keswick situation and our home situation. Some people have been honest enough to admit to me this week that the convention is rather like a filling station for them. You take in litres of spiritual fuel during July and then for the rest of the year you're gradually running down. And some of you have been running on empty. How can we go on, consistently living the Christian life, in what might be more difficult circumstances?

Tough times

Paul was leaving Timothy in a very difficult situation. Paul says, 'You know, Timothy, that everyone in Asia has deserted me' (1:15). Just a few years previously, Luke records that through Paul's ministry, all of the Jews and the Greeks who lived in the province of Asia had heard the word of the Lord and many had believed and they no doubt saw Paul and his companions as their fathers in the faith (Acts 19). But what a change. Tough times for Paul, facing death, dealing with the massive disappointment of this defection. Tough times for Timothy; isolated there in Ephesus, because he remains faithful to God and Paul, separated from his great mentor. Paul probably had only days to live and that would have been very clear as he read the letter.

Stand firm

So what does Paul have to say to Timothy, to encourage him at such a tough time? What will help Timothy go on for God in what is clearly a very difficult situation? First of all, Paul does expect Timothy to stand firm (2:1). He's not expecting him to join the crowd of defectors. Verse 1 – 'You then, my son, be strong'. This can also be translated, 'But as for you …' 'Timothy, I expect you to stand against the tide.' How can he do it? '… be strong in the grace that is in Christ Jesus.' Paul uses exactly the same word in Ephesians 6 and verse 10. 'Finally, be strong' – then he adds these words, 'in the Lord and in His mighty power.'

We all know the meaning of the word grace, it's unmerited favour. When we were utterly unable to help ourselves, sinners dead in our sins, cut off from God, we received His grace. That's why we're Christians, not because of our resolve or commitment, but because of His grace. That same grace, that same unmerited help of Christ, is there to strengthen us for daily Christian living. John Stott says: 'It's not only for salvation that we are dependent on grace. We're dependent on grace for service as well.'

I'm particularly encouraged that it's Timothy to whom Paul gives this exhortation because throughout the epistles, Paul seems to be encouraging this man to stand firm. 'God did not give us a spirit of timidity, but a spirit of power, of love and of self-discipline' (1:7).' Many of us this week have been challenged to share our faith much more boldly. We've been reminded of eternal realities. This exhortation is given in the context of Timothy using his spiritual gifts – look at the previous verse. 'Fan into flame the gift of God which is in you'. *The Message* translates that: Timothy, 'God doesn't want us to be shy with His gifts but bold, loving and sensible.' 'Endure hardship with us' (2:3), and there are many other references which show that Timothy was not naturally resilient. Here's Paul leaving him in an incredibly difficult situation. He knows it's going to involve Timothy in hardship but he's confident that he can stand strong because of the grace that is in Christ Jesus. The grace that is in Christ Jesus is available to all who are in Christ Jesus. It was available to Timothy, it's available to us. Remember how Paul goes on in Ephesians 6, to use those words: 'the grace and mighty power of Christ, is available to us all.'

The mighty power of Christ

Pause for one moment to think about that mighty power. From time to time in the life of Christ, when He was on this earth, that power would break forth. As the detachment of soldiers come to arrest Him, and make it clear who they're after, Jesus says: 'I am He.' They draw back and fall to the ground. In the original, just one word from the lips of Jesus leave armed soldiers on their backs, helpless. Whatever situation, easy or difficult, we may be moving into, we have the grace, the mighty power that is in Christ Jesus. That's a challenge as well as an encouragement, because in that grace Paul expects Timothy to stand. We can be very quick to excuse ourselves as Christians. 'We're only human. These are very tough times and my church isn't up to much.' But there are actually no excuses because of the grace that is in Christ Jesus. Peter puts it like this – 'We have all that we need for life and godliness.' So with that encouragement, Paul gives Timothy six little pictures which will help him to realise what's ahead and what he's going to need if he's going to stand firm.

First of all we've got the picture of the soldier (verse 4) calling us to wholehearted devotion. Then the athlete (verse 5) reminding us of the discipline required to run the race to the end. Verse 6 introduces us to the farmer and the sheer hard graft so often required in Christian living and service. We have the grace that is in Christ Jesus, but that does not deliver us from the need to work hard at this business of Christian living. A diligent workman (verses 14-19) underlines that point. The specific work in mind here is the work of the teacher, correctly handling the word of truth. I'm conscious that there are many preachers here. Are we putting the work in? We need that mighty power in our preaching. What about the diligent preparation?

Then we've got the clean vessel (verses 20,21) reminding us that all our work, however diligent, will be ruined unless the vessel, the worker, by the power of Christ, keeps his life pure and holy. Finally, the Lord's bondservant (verses 24,25), a challenging picture of the gentleness required in the Christian worker. These six pictures build up into a powerful image of what will be required of Timothy, if he's going to remain faithful and fruitful, in the most trying of circumstances. In the middle of those six pictures we've got the six verses that I want to concentrate on (verses 8-13). They contain two examples for Timothy to follow, one certainty for him to hold onto and some inspiring and challenging truths.

Remember Jesus

It's so easy in the Christian life to get our eyes off Jesus. We find ourselves living the Christian life to satisfy other people – for the church, or even for ourselves, the sense of fulfilment that we receive. Remember Him tomorrow and maybe on Monday morning. Remember that we're living for Jesus, for His sake, for His glory. Remember, however tough it might get, He is worthy. Remember the exhortation of Hebrews, chapter 3, 'Fix your thoughts on Jesus'. Moses sets us the example. Moses had some very hard choices and maybe you've got some hard decisions. For Moses, it was the palace or the desert, acceptance with royalty or the privation of the slave life. Again, Hebrews tells us, Moses 'regarded disgrace for the sake of Christ as of greater value than the treasures of Egypt'.

I was listening to a man recently, speaking on the second coming. He said how easy it is to forget that the second coming of Jesus is about Jesus. It's not primarily about millenniums, tribulations, Israel or the anti-Christ: it's about Jesus. 'Timothy, everyone else may be turning away, but I expect you to stand against the tide, however tough the circumstances, and I expect you to do it by the power and for the sake of Jesus. And as you keep your eyes on Him, remember two things: He was raised from the dead, and He is descended from David.'

'Raised from the dead': this reminds us of His divinity. He was declared the Son of God with power, by His resurrection from the dead, underlining again that mighty power which is available to us. But He also descended from David, reminding us of His humanity. Some of you may be plunged back into real problems. Remember that there's Someone in heaven Who is descended from David, Who's been tempted and tested in every way that we will ever be, sin apart. There's understanding in heaven, He understands our struggles more than we do. If I can put this reverently, when Satan turned up the heat of his temptations against Christ, he just kept turning the knob, time, time, time again, and the resistance of Christ, according to Scripture, against those temptations was 'unto blood'. He never gave an inch. He felt everything that Satan had to throw at Him but never took one half pace back. We've never felt that heat that He felt; we've always given way before the intensity has reached its height. Remember Jesus Christ.

Imitate Paul

The second example is Paul himself. This statement about Jesus, that He was raised from the dead and descended from David, is a very succinct expression of Paul's gospel. Paul says: It's for this gospel that I'm suffering – 'even to the point of being chained like a criminal'(verse 9). Paul is calling Timothy to stand firm against the raging tide. He knows it's going to involve suffering but Paul himself has already taken a similar stand. As he writes, he's suffering the consequences. Paul is not writing from the comfort of his study but as someone who will very soon be martyred for his faith.

Mentoring

Timothy had an example, a mentor. How such people are needed in today's church. We know there's an increasing weariness of people whose lives don't match their words. People are looking for those who really do walk the talk, and Timothy had found such a man. The grace that is in Christ Jesus meant everything to Timothy. But Paul meant a lot to him as well, and it was mutual. Remember how Paul wrote to the Philippians – 'I have no one else like Timothy.' I hope you've got a Timothy or the equivalent in your life. I have – two or three people that I'm ready regularly to open up my life to, and they with me, to share everything together so that we can grow together in Christ. Younger people, and younger believers particularly, are looking for examples; for models of what commitment to Christ means. I wonder if that's God's call on some of our lives. I'm convinced that evangelism is not the biggest problem in the church today. I think it's discipleship. The biblical model of discipleship is Jesus with the Twelve around Him and they're not only drinking in His teaching – they're watching the model of His life. 'One of his disciples said to him, "Lord, teach us to pray"'(Lk. 11:1). See the motivation of an example?

Timothy had his suffering mentor, Paul. But this suffering, Paul knows, is not without purpose. 'I endure everything for the sake of the elect, that they too may obtain the salvation that is in Christ Jesus, with eternal glory' (verse 10). Paul doesn't mean there's some sort of redemptive power in his suffering, he's stating what has proven to be a fact throughout the history of the church – the progress of the gospel goes hand in hand with suffering. Latest estimates tell us that three thousand people every hour decide to follow Christ in our world. It's a record for any time in the history of the church. We're also having more people martyred for the faith than ever before. I've been telling some of you of amazing opportunities in India today. Indian Christian leaders tell me you can trace much of what's happening in India today back to the horrific martyrdom of Australian missionary Graham Staines and his two young sons. 'Timothy! I'm asking you to stand firm in difficult times, I know it will involve suffering, but take heart, I'm suffering here in this prison but I know that my present suffering is leading to the progress of the gospel.'

God's word is not chained

There are two examples to inspire Timothy but what is the instrument that God uses to keep His church moving forward in all circumstances?

Look at the one certainty which Timothy has to encourage him. 'I am suffering to the point of being chained like a criminal. But God's word is not chained' (verse 9). There are many examples you could give from Scripture for that. Philippians chapter 1:12 – Paul is assuring worried Macedonian believers, '... what has happened to me has really served to advance the gospel.' One of the specific fruits of Paul's imprisonment was most of the brothers in the Lord in Rome 'have been encouraged to speak the word of God more ... fearlessly.' You can try and snuff out the word through persecution, through criticism, but you'll never succeed.

Napoleon realised the power of the Bible. He wrote: 'The Bible is no mere book, it's a living creature. It has power to conquer all who oppose it.' Martin Luther, the great reformer, said towards the end of his life: 'I have done nothing. The word has done and accomplished everything.' Sometimes the power of the Bible is experienced in surprising ways. I heard a couple of weeks ago about a man who'd been living rough. He was walking along a promenade and a man was preaching and offering New Testaments. The man looked at the New Testament and saw the very fine paper and thought, that would be excellent for rolling cigarettes. So he took a copy and was converted through reading the papers he was rolling. 'Timothy, tough times ahead. But one thing I do know. Nothing can stop the spread of the living word of God.' This week we've experienced the power of the word. Let's be committed to communicating that word wherever God make take us in the days ahead.

Inspirational teaching

Paul places four truths before Timothy (verses 11-13). Firstly, 'If we died with Him, we will also live with Him'. Paul is writing here of death to self, that daily dying to our own selfish agendas. In the context in which Paul and Timothy found themselves, death to self would also mean death to safety. It was possibly too late for Paul although even at this late hour, if he'd renounced Christ, he might have preserved his life. But for Timothy, a different story: Just keep your head down. Back off… but no. We know Paul's final word to him: 'Preach the word, Timothy! Be prepared in season, when it's convenient, and out of season, when it's totally inconvenient.'

Here's one of the great truths of Jesus of which we must remind ourselves. I wonder if we really believe it? I find myself having to repent sometimes many times that I have not lived as though I believed this simple fundamental truth; the way to life is death. To use the words of Jesus, if we want to save our lives, we must lose them. But if we make that decision, if we choose to lose our lives for His sake, we will find them. In Bonhoeffer's famous words, 'When Christ calls us, He calls us to come and die.' That's the truth of Jesus – 'Come and die if you want to really live.' It's no easy call.

Endurance

The second truth Paul places before him: 'If we endure, we will also reign with him.' Faithfulness includes the decision to keep on struggling when the going isn't easy, when others might be giving up the fight, as was the case with Timothy. It needs constant endurance if I'm going to win the battle with my flesh. It was D.L. Moody who said, 'I have more trouble with D.L. Moody than ever other man I've ever met.' The result of that struggle, if we endure, will be seen both in this life and the next. If we die with Him, we'll live with Him. If we endure with Him, we'll see the fruit in this life. And, says Paul, 'we will also reign with Him'. Great encouragement for Timothy and for us, whatever the difficulties ahead might be.

If we disown Him …

There's challenge here as well as warning. If we disown Him, truth number three, He will disown us. This call to endure is surrounded by promises and encouragement but we would be untrue to Scripture if we didn't face the warnings head on. Remember the words of Jesus;:'Whoever denies Me before men, I also will deny him before my Father in heaven' (Mt. 10:32). Some profess the faith, enjoy the benefits of the believing community, but ultimately prove to be false believers. Scripture calls us to examine ourselves. This call to self-examination can, and often is, used by the devil. It's used to trouble true believers so that they never enjoy the peace of God in their hearts. Don't allow Satan, the great thief, to rob you of your assurance and your joy – that's a tragedy. But there's also a danger of what Bonhoeffer used to call 'cheap grace'. Let me just quote from Bonhoeffer, one paragraph:

> Grace is represented as the church's inexhaustible treasury from which He showers blessings with generous hands without asking questions or fixing limits. You see, it's grace without price; grace without cost. We imagine that the essence of grace is that the account has all been paid in advance. And because it's been paid everything can be had for nothing. Since the cost was infinite, the possibilities of using it and spending it are infinite; after all, what would grace be if it were not cheap. So cheap grace becomes the preaching of forgiveness without requiring repentance. It becomes baptism without church discipline, it becomes communion without confession. Cheap grace is grace without discipleship; grace without the cross, grace without Jesus Christ, living and incarnate.

Let me be very honest. Grace without the cross, grace without discipleship, is a disgrace. Philip Yancey relates this incident. Not long ago, he sat in a restaurant and listened to yet another variation on a familiar theme. 'A good friend of mine, I'll call him Daniel, had decided to leave his wife after fifteen years of marriage. He'd found someone younger, prettier, someone who "makes me feel alive like I haven't felt for years". Daniel, a Christian, knew well the personal and moral consequences of what he was about to do. His decision to leave would inflict permanent damage on his wife and three children. Even so, he said, the force pulling him towards the young woman was too strong to resist.' Yancey says, 'I listened to his story with sadness and grief. Then during the dessert course he dropped a bombshell. "The reason, Philip, I wanted to see you tonight was to ask you a question. Do you think God can forgive something as awful as I am about to do?"'

Let's be clear. The Scriptures never offer the sort of security that allows anyone to adopt such a cavalier attitude towards sin. You might say, but what about the fourth truth? 'If we are faithless, He will remain faithful … He cannot deny Himself.' Ah, people say, in the end it'll be OK. God is faithful even when we are faithless. And it is true, Scripture affirms that God will preserve the weakest, failing, faltering believer. But be sure for anyone with a careless, carefree attitude towards sin, there is no comfort here.

Commentators divide over how this passage should be interpreted. Is this a word of comfort or is it a word of warning? Some argue that the faithfulness to which Paul refers here is God's faithfulness to his warnings. And if that's the case, what's Paul is actually saying is something like this: If we disown Christ, He will disown us. If we are faithless, He will remain faithful to that promise to disown us.

As we come to the Lord's table this evening, we come with absolute confidence in the finished work of Christ. We plead the merit of His blood, not the merit of our faithfulness or our endurance. We bring all our failure and all our weakness with us to His cross. We cannot come with such confidence if we're deliberately continuing with some sinful practice in our lives. Paul's words, 'Remember Jesus Christ' and continuing in deliberate sin, they just don't dovetail, do they? We must respond to the warnings of Scripture.

So how can we go on walking consistently with Christ, even when the circumstances are tough? What does Paul do? Very simply, he points Timothy to Jesus. Remember Jesus Christ, His grace, His power. Remember the power of His word. Remember the privilege of dying, living and reigning with Him. And we trust that the result of Keswick 2002 will be that it has brought people to Jesus. I know it's brought some to trust Him for the first time and we rejoice in that. I trust it's brought all of us to examine our relationship with Him. As we move on from this convention, may those words ring around our minds: remember Jesus Christ.

Brought into the Kingdom

by Liam Goligher

LIAM GOLIGHER

Converted at an early age, Liam felt a strong call to preach at the age of twelve, primarily through the showing of a Billy Graham film. He started preaching to cows and graduated to people at the age of fifteen. After studying in Belfast, he pastored churches in Ireland, Canada and his native Scotland. Outside the local church, he has been involved in student ministry in the UK and eastern Europe. Since 2000, he has been Senior Minister of Duke Street Church in Richmond. With five children, Liam's main recreational activity is that of taxi driver. Any spare time he does have, he likes to use for swimming, fishing, walking the dog or going to the movies.

Brought into the Kingdom
Luke chapter 15

Introduction

This chapter of Luke's gospel is so well known to us that we probably
have forgotten what the impact of it is. It seems to me that there are
two kinds of people for whom this chapter has particular relevance.
There are those who do not yet have a relationship with God. Maybe
you don't want a relationship with God, maybe you're not sure that if
you did, that God would particularly want a relationship with you.
There's another kind of person who would claim to have had a relationship with God over many, many years. I guarantee that some of you
who say you have a relationship with God, as we go through this
passage, will discover you don't have a relationship with God at all.

The two religions

This chapter is about grace. There are only two kinds of religion in
the world. One is a religion of performance, and the other is a religion of grace. A religion of performance can be defined like this; it's
all about earned acceptance, conditionally given to worthy achievers.
Some of you were brought up in that kind of environment: acceptance at home, affection at home, approval at home, was always given

on that basis – it was always earned. You had to do your homework, to tidy your room, to achieve well at sport, to win prizes, to be a good boy or girl, and then you were given favour, approval and acceptance. That attitude has pervaded every aspect of your life ever since. It affects your relationship with your spouse, your children, your employers or your employees. It affects the way you perceive God and the way you perceive religion. You're into a religion of performance. But then there is the religion of grace, and grace can be defined as undeserved acceptance, freely given, to unworthy sinners. Both of these religions find their expression in this great parable of prodigal grace. The word 'prodigal' means wastefully extravagant. These parables in Luke 15 are about grace that is careless, lavish, free. Grace that comes unexpectedly, undeservedly, and without restraint, to those who are not expecting it. I want to pick our way through these stories and to show you how God is gracious to us. I feel I need to persuade some of you this evening that God is a gracious God and that He wants to be gracious to you.

God is gracious in the way in which He loves us

We need to see that in Jesus today. All of Luke 15 is spoken as an answer to an accusation by the Pharisees and the scribes (verse 2) that Jesus was welcoming sinners and eating with them. Really conspicuous sinners were coming near to Jesus and listening to Him. He was making space for them; encouraging them to come and stay and eat with Him. The religious leaders began grumbling and accusing Him. They're challenging the Lord Jesus, saying: 'Who do You think You are?'

The answer Jesus gives is absolutely spectacular. He might as well have set off an atomic bomb among those religious leaders. We're so familiar with it, some of us churchgoers, that we miss the astonishing force of this answer. Here we are in a Jewish village somewhere. It's round about lunchtime and somebody has opened their home, pulled back the shutters so it's open to the street. In that home, Jesus is having lunch. Some of these notorious people are coming in and having lunch alongside the Lord Jesus. The religious leaders, on the outside, are looking on, observing the kind of people that Jesus is mixing with. They start to grumble. Jesus hears and He answers with a couple of parables. So it's no big deal; just a lunch, a few pious people who can't agree with each other, a religious squabble, a few stories – in another part of the world there's a major war going on and many, many thousands are dying. This is a small thing. Right?

God is accessible

Then you listen more carefully to these stories. Suddenly, it dawns on you – this Jesus is saying that the God of heaven, the God before Whom all the angels bow down in worship, this God is at this very table, in these very words, in this very man, reaching into the lives of these very people. He's bringing them to repentance, welcoming them into His own possession and leading them to cause heaven to rejoice. That's what's going on at that lunch table. Suddenly you realise that a battle anywhere in the world is nothing compared to what is going on here. Here is a man claiming that the habitation of God and the habitation of man are intersecting. God is being revealed and is actually acting in this world and showing Himself – and that is the most important thing in the world to know. God is accessible. The scribes and Pharisees are grumbling that Jesus is eating with tax collectors and sinners and Jesus says: 'the love of God in heaven has entered the world through Me and is seeking and finding what belongs to God and is now lost.'

In these three stories, He says to the people around Him, 'My receiving sinners and eating with them is like a shepherd leaving his ninety-nine sheep and going out to find the one lost sheep. Then, when he brings it back, bringing his friends together and having a party. My receiving sinners and eating with them is like a woman lighting a lamp, sweeping her house and searching diligently for that one coin that meant a day's wages to her, and when she finds it, bringing her friends together for a party.'

Heaven rejoices

Some of those scribes and Pharisees were thinking, 'What's He getting at?' and some of you are thinking, 'Where is the connection? How is this like a neighbourhood party?' Jesus spells it out for us in verse 7 and verse 10: 'I tell you that in the same way there will be more joy in heaven over one sinner who repents than over ninety-nine righteous people who need no repentance.' 'In the same way, there is joy in the presence of God over one sinner who repents' (verse 10).

God has a universe to run, galaxies to uphold and governments to rule in His providence. But you won't find much in the Bible that says that all heaven rejoices over orbits of the stars or global conferences or World Cups but you will read in the Bible, over and over again, that there is joy in heaven over one sinner who repents. God is gracious in the way He loves you, as an individual, whoever you are, whatever your background.

God is gracious in the way He seeks us

God's grace is seeking grace. He searches relentlessly till He finds what is lost. You see that demonstrated in these three parables: there's the story of a shepherd who's lost a sheep and he leaves the sheep and out he goes looking for it. Here is this woman out looking for her lost coin. It's a very personal search. Henri Nouwen in his book *The Return of the Prodigal* reminds us how personal this search is. 'God rejoices,' he says, 'not because the problems of the world have been solved, not because all human pain and suffering have come to an end, nor because thousands of people have been converted and are now praising Him for His goodness. No, God rejoices because one of His children who was lost has been found.'

He is out seeking, and you see this same personal search in the third parable in the sequence: the parable of the prodigal son. Did you ever notice when you read that story, how the father is already there look-ing for the boy? He is neglecting his duties, neglecting his estate, neglecting his home because he is so focused. Every day he is out there and he is scanning the horizon, he is searching, looking for his lost boy. God's grace is a seeking grace. That's why Jesus said He had come to seek and save the lost – it is a personal business for Him. It was that kind of seeking grace that sent Jesus into the world. He told us that Himself. 'I have come to seek and save' – the whole purpose of His coming, His incarnation, was to seek and save. The whole reason why He left heaven and put skin on, made Himself vulnerable to where we were, died for our sins, as our substitute taking the penalty on Himself – the whole reason behind that is that He is passionate in his desire to seek and save those who are lost. He has been looking for you. The grace of God takes the initiative. He doesn't wait for you, He moves towards you.

God is gracious in the way He welcomes us

Luke uses that word in verse 2: 'This man welcomes sinners.' That word, wherever else it's used in Luke's gospel, always means to eagerly await or look for something. In Luke 2:25, Simeon was eagerly awaiting the consolation of Israel. In Luke 2:38, Anna, the prophetess in the temple was eagerly awaiting the redemption of Israel. In Luke 12:36, Jesus says, 'Be like those who are eagerly awaiting the return of the master.' So when we read in Luke 15 verse 2, 'This man welcomes sinners, and eats with them', what we are to understand is that that is not a passive thing. He is looking out for and preparing Himself to welcome those who come back to Him.

The prodigal father

Jesus' most famous story, the third one of this trilogy, is of a son who led a wasteful and extravagant life. Actually the story is not about the extravagant son, it's about the extravagant father, the prodigal father, who is prodigal in the grace that he shows towards this son. The younger son comes to his dad and he wants what's coming to him, and his dad gives him half of all that he possesses. Actually the younger son only deserved, upon the death of the father, to have a third of the inheritance so there is wasteful extravagance there. The son squanders his inheritance. Then the son comes 'to his senses', it says. He reckons that he had wasted everything, but that the father remained the father he had always known and reckons that if he goes back the father will receive him even if it's only to be a servant.

God's compassion

It's then that we read in verse 20, that when 'he was still a long way off, his father saw him and was filled with compassion'. There is something in Almighty God like that. Jesus is saying to you, 'God is like this.' If one of your children or one of your friends have ever really hurt you and you've seen them in a mess or you've seen them hurt, and there has risen up within you a sense of compassion, then you understand God. There is something in Almighty God that is moved with compassion for people.

Verse 20 again, 'he ran'. In the Middle East, a middle-aged man, the owner of a significant estate, with servants at his beck and call, had decorum to maintain; such people to do not run. But here is a man who puts aside his dignity because of the joy he has at seeing his son come home. Verse 20 again: 'He ran to his son, he embraced him and he kissed him, threw his arms around him and he kissed him.' See the welcome that God gives. Jesus uses emotion-laden language to describe what God is like here. He does it quite deliberately – He wants you to know this is what God is like towards you. He welcomes those who come.

Then the son makes his confession in verse 22. The father says to his slave, 'Quickly, bring out the best robe and put it on him.' He welcomes him back not to slavery or even servanthood but sonship; welcomes him back right into the family, puts the ring on his finger, brings out the fatted calf, throws a party – there is gladness in the heart of God as He welcomes those who come to Him. Martin Luther once said, 'If I could believe that God was not angry with me I would stand on my head for joy.' The Bible says it – 'this son of mine was dead and has come back to life again.' All this is to illustrate this principle: God is gracious in the way He welcomes us.

God is gracious in the way He defends us

From verse 25 of this chapter, there is a negative side to all this talk of grace. In verse 12 this parable of the prodigal grace of the father takes a turn. Instead of answering the question 'Why is it that Jesus is eating with tax collectors and sinners?', the question now is: 'What does it mean that the Pharisees and the scribes are not eating with them?' That's what the last part of this parable is about – the grace of God being a disruptive force, something that offends our sense of justice. It does seem unjust, that such an extravagant party should be thrown for such a waster of a boy. It seems unjust that the faithful older brother is not celebrated in the same way as his wayward younger sibling. Clearly the prodigal nature of God's grace disrupts us because of how it is given – extravagantly.

The older brother

The older brother in Jesus' story provocatively gives voice to that sense of outrage. The text tells us he was not willing to go in for the celebrations. What kind of father was this? What kind of behaviour would this kind of action encourage? What kind of virtue would this grow in the heart of this wayward boy? Had the father not considered that if you treat people like this who waste as much and then just welcome them back – as if nothing's happened – the social order would fall apart, wouldn't it?

Here's his railing against his father. 'For so many years I have slaved for you and I've not neglected any command of yours, yet you never gave me a kid that I might be merry with my friends, and when this son of yours came, who devoured your wealth with whores, you killed the fatted calf for him.' He's saying: 'It's not fair. I'm angry.' He thinks he's been treated unfairly. Yet, like the Pharisees and the religious leaders who were the audience for the story, the older brother does not listen to the gracious words of the father. Listen to how the father defends the boy, the wayward one. God's defence of us does not rest on our worthiness or our unworthiness, but on His own sovereign decision to show free unconditional love and acceptance towards the unworthy sinner. Period. The father doesn't get into an argument saying, 'He wasn't all bad. There were good bits to him as well as bad bits.' All he says to his boy is, 'This is what I want to do for him.' These words go straight to the heart of what Christianity is.

Slaving for God

Listen to that elder brother. For some people, this is your relationship with God. 'Look,' he says to the father, 'All these years I've been

slaving for you.' Get that word: 'slaving'? How does he see his relationship with God? He goes on, 'I've never neglected a command of
yours.' How does he see his dad? As a master giving orders? Does he
see himself simply as a slave paying obedience?

That isn't Christianity. That isn't a Christian life. That isn't the good
news message of the gospel. It dishonours God, Jesus is saying, to treat
Him like a master in need of slave labour. As Jesus says of Himself,
'The Son of Man did not come to be served but to serve and to give
His life as a ransom for many.' When Jesus came, He didn't hang out
a 'Help Wanted' sign – He hung up a 'Help Available' sign. He was the
doctor and He had the cure. He was not an employer with a labour
shortage, looking for people to sign up. The Pharisees and the scribes
couldn't see that because they'd got a totally different mind-set.

'For so many years I've been slaving for you.' Test yourself here –
do you think he's got a point? Maybe something's happened to you in
your life and maybe you've lost your job or you've been overlooked
for promotion. Maybe your health has deteriorated. Maybe you're saying to yourself: 'This is not fair. What is God playing at that this has
happened to me? I've been involved in church all these years and I've
worked so hard and doesn't God ever pay any attention to what we
do for Him?' Don't you hear that you're talking like the elder brother, as if your relationship with God was a kind of *quid pro quo* kind
of relationship, a business of slaving and serving? What were you doing
all that work for? So that He'd give you good health? So that you'd
avoid all the bad stuff that happens to people in a fallen world where
health goes, relationships break down and circumstances turn bad?

Let me spell out what happens when we start thinking like this. We
start disconnecting ourselves from the needy and the sinners. I was in
a church once where some people in leadership complained to me
about the new people who were being converted, because they were
bringing their baggage from their non-Christian past with them into
the church. They said to me, 'This church was a great church before
you came and brought all these people.' They didn't like the fact that
these people rolled up their sleeves and wanted to get into the business of getting the gospel out. It makes us blamers. Look at verse 30,
'this son of yours', not 'my lost brother'. Just like Adam saying to God,

'this woman that You gave me led me to sin.' When we relate to God as a slave to master on the basis of our hard work, we'll even blame God for the mess-ups in the world.

Notice how the father approaches this man. The father does for the second brother what he did for the first: he came out looking for him. It's one of those horrible family moments. Somebody is in a foul mood and they won't come to the table. This is deeper and far worse – what does Dad do? He goes out looking for the one who's not coming to the table. He doesn't holler from the distance, or command the boy to come, he doesn't send his wife out to get him – which is what most of us guys would do! He comes out face to face. The father came out and began entreating him. What was the word the boy used about his dad? 'Your commands; I do everything you command me!' Here's the father, he's not commanding him, he's entreating him, he is pleading with him.

'My child'

After the son's bitter complaint, the father responds in verse 31 and his first words are all-important: 'My child'. Not 'my servant' or 'my slave' but 'my child'. He exposes the distortion that is deep in his son's heart. He doesn't have to argue the point, it would lead him nowhere, but emphasises in that word what the essence of that relationship should have been. 'My child, you have always been with me.' Or 'You are always with me', literally.

Here we have exposed the void in this boy's heart. He lived in the house with the father but found no satisfaction with the father. Some of the most ominous words in the elder brother's mouth are these: 'You never gave me a kid so that I might be merry with my friends.' Here's the heir of the estate; he has at his disposal flocks of goats and herds of cattle, a father who is manifestly kind and gracious, so what do these hard words mean?

They are the words of a person for whom the grace and glory of the father has ceased to be his treasure. They are the words of a person whose heart is with his friends outside the family and who feels locked in to the father's table when he would really rather be with others. It may very well be that you are in the home but the Father is not your treasure. The Father is not the One you love. You don't have a relationship with the Father and very often that's exposed when something goes wrong and you really see where your heart lies. Frankly, if you could, if circumstances would just work out for you and without losing face, your family relationships, your friends and all the rest of it, if you could just get out of church, that would be great. But you can't, and you feel locked in. Or all that you're doing for church, you're doing for work's sake. You don't have relationship with your Father any more. You are as lost at home as the other boy was lost far away and you need to come to your senses, every bit as much as the wild boy did, so that you can come back home to your Father, who says to you, 'all that is mine is yours.'

It's a gift

It's not a wage to be earned. It's a gift to be taken. 'All that is mine is yours, if only you'll come in with the sinners.' That's what Jesus is saying to those Pharisees and religious leaders – it's all there for you if only you will come in with the sinners. If only you'll recognise that you need grace, that a relationship with God, acceptance with God, is not a matter of works, of trying, of performance, of 'do better, work harder' but is a matter of sheer grace, a gift that He offers you freely in Christ.

Maybe you're the wild son. You've wandered far away from God and wonder if God will have you back. Let me tell you, God's doesn't say 'Measure up!' He says, 'Come on into the party.' Maybe you're like the older brother; it offends your sense of justice that God will forgive somebody who's wasted their life and let them get ahead of you in church circles. Maybe your whole view of what you do as a Christian is in terms of labour, work, effort, because you really don't know the Father. The word to you is 'Come on in with the sinners. Receive the grace of the Father that He so freely, so lavishly, so profoundly, so extravagantly, wants to pour into your life.'

Behold your King

by Rob Warner

ROB WARNER

Rob Warner is the pastoral leader of 'Kairos – Church from Scratch.' He is married to Claire and they have two teenage sons. Before becoming a Baptist minister, he worked in publishing with Hodder & Stoughton. Rob is a widely travelled speaker and has given daily Bible Readings at many conferences, including Spring Harvest and Easter People. His Leadership Show can be heard weekly on Premier Radio and he writes regularly for the *Christian Herald* and *Christianity+Renewal*. His books include *21st Century Church* and *Walking with God*. He is a trustee of the Evangelical Alliance and Renovare UK. Rob's longing is to encourage churches for the unchurched and the de-churched.

Behold your King
Isaiah 40:1 – 31

Understand our world

Around the world the church of Jesus Christ is growing rapidly in every continent except one. This vulnerability in Europe, particularly western Europe, was brought home to me when I was leading a church in south-east London. We invited in the local primary school after we'd redeveloped the premises. This was entirely an excuse to talk to them about Jesus in an appropriately educational context. In order to explain something of our priorities, before they came into the room where we met to worship, we invited the children to identify what they expected to see there. We already knew that two-thirds of them had never been in any kind of church building. Nonetheless they thought they knew what would be there. They said there would be pillars, a pulpit, big candles and probably one or two statues ... and I was delighted to know that none of them were going to be found. Not because those things are wrong, but because the children thought they knew what church was. They already knew it wasn't for them and we wanted to try to surprise them.

We noted that as they walked up the stairs, the teachers and the assistants were telling them to be quiet, because one of the curious

traditions that has grown up in our culture is that God disapproves of
children. There is no evidence in the Scriptures that God has particularly sensitive ears or that He disapproves of children. Those children
thought they knew what church was about, the adults who came with
them thought they knew what God was about and in both cases they
knew what they thought it was about was not for them.

I don't know whether those who come to Keswick are regular
frequenters of betting shops. I've never been in one myself. I know that
if I went into a betting shop, I wouldn't know where to stand, what to
do, what to say … I have a sneaking suspicion that the people there
would say things to me and I wouldn't have a clue what they were
talking about. We need to understand that in our kind of world, for
many non-Christians today, to come into a church is to enter an
alien environment. Church is as incomprehensible to the average non-
churchgoer today as a betting shop is to an average Keswick evangelical.
Church conveys an image of God and sometimes it's not surprising that
people are put off because we're very good at putting people off.
Sometimes our churches are very good at advertising a God no
one wants and Christians are very good at commending a God no one
wants. Jesus said, 'I come to give life in all its fullness,' but the church
decided that grumbling and committees were much more fun instead.

Here is your God

We start not with our image of God, our ideas about God, our
church's way of traditionally expressing God but with the Scriptures
and the self-revelation of God. Supremely we do that in Jesus Christ,
the definitive revelation of God. But here in this climactic chapter of
Isaiah's prophesies, we have Isaiah describing things about God that
we need to hear and that we need to commend to others.

First I need to give you the setting: in Isaiah 6, Isaiah is told that he
has a ministry of declaring God's judgement. The first time I read the
book of Isaiah, I found the first thirty-nine chapters profoundly
depressing, because their main theme is God's resolve to bring judgement. Suddenly, in that context, this new note is struck in Isaiah 40.

Isaiah 6, severe judgement, Isaiah 36 to 39, they're saved from the Assyrians; the Assyrians are swept away in such terms that Isaiah can only say, 'That was a work of God.' But even as they are rescued, Isaiah hints they're already doomed by the coming conquest of the Babylonians. From Isaiah 40, it speaks beyond that time: the Babylonians come, they destroy the walls and the temple, they take people away to serve the Babylonian empire. But from Isaiah 40 it's a new day that's promised; the day of returning to the land, of God's new favour. That's the setting.

A time of endings

Israel had been powerful for a brief interlude in the time of David and Solomon but now those times have come to an end. The Davidic line, having a king on the throne in Jerusalem, had come to an end. Isaiah promises a future king, and we understand in those prophecies, he speaks of Jesus. But the time of Davidic kings comes to an end. From the time of Jerusalem to the time of the Babylonians, there was a close link between temple and state, the two were close together and it would never be quite like that again. Both in terms of their national status and in terms of the status of their religion, Isaiah is speaking of a time of endings.

It should not be difficult for us to identify parallels in western Europe today, and there are two options that we can't seize just as Isaiah doesn't allow them to be options for Israel to consider. We can't go on with business as usual, pretending that the church is the equivalent of the orchestra on the Titanic. Nor can we say, 'Let's go back to the good old days.' The task of the church is not to be a museum of yesterday's religion, but to provide mission centres to the world of today and tomorrow. We have to move forward. As Isaiah brings good news, he sets it in that context of endings. He says, learn to accept it! Some things have gone. I think we need to do the same. The church can't say to the state any more, 'That's wrong – stop doing it!' We have to learn wisdom to be the people of God in new and unpredictable territory.

Isaiah prophesies comfort, hope and care (verses 1-11). In verse 2 he says, 'The days of hard service have been completed.' There is a season of judgement, God's wrath being worked out on the pages of human history. Jeremiah spoke, prophesying into that same period of judgement and said that there were false prophets who proclaimed peace where there was no peace – because it was a season of judgement. It sometimes seems to me that we live in days when some proclaim success when there is little hard evidence to back it up. There is a season of judgement. But here Isaiah says that season of judgement is brought to an end by the favour of God.

God is coming in glory

The hard service is completed and God wants a motorway built (verses 3-5). Isaiah here is not prophesying motorway building in the age of the motor car. He's describing what they did in the ancient world when an emperor conquered new territory. You built a special processional highway. It had to be absolutely straight and level and then with all those that demonstrated the glory of the emperor they processed down this triumphant way. Isaiah says in an age when the forces that opposed Israel were very powerful, when if anyone was going to have a triumphal procession it was not going to be the people of God, when they knew their vulnerability, not their strength, Isaiah says, 'Build that motorway, because your God is coming in glory!'

We're told because God is coming in glory, Isaiah is meant to cry out 'Good news!' He says, 'What shall I cry?' He's given news that at first doesn't seem very positive at all. 'Cry out that people are like grass, like the flowers of the field, and the breath of God breathes and they wither and die.' This is a picture of summer in a hot country. The hot winds blow and all that's grown up following the Spring rains is suddenly burned to the ground. Isaiah says, 'I want you to understand that that's the glory and the frailty of the human condition. There's something wonderful to celebrate before God about being alive, but the breath of God blows upon us like the wind of summer and our life is taken.'

The same breath that can take life from us is the breath that breathes revelation (verse 7). The word of our God stands for ever. That's why over the years of a convention like this, many have preached the word of God and been forgotten but it's the word of

God that endures. The wise preacher is more concerned that you might take something away from the word of God. Isaiah speaks of a confident declaration of the God of hope (verses 8-10). He is coming, He is glorious. We can have confidence whatever our context.

More glorious than the emperor

There's a contrast again (verse 11). Verse 9 and 10, it's like the herald of the emperor. The herald announces the glory and in comes the emperor. He's more glorious than the most glorious of emperors, He's more tender than the most tender of shepherds (verse 11). Sometimes on the television you see a line of people being introduced, usually to the United States' president because they let the media have more access than our media usually have. You see the president going along shaking people's hands, and somebody else whispering in the president's ear, telling them who they are, what they do and what he should say to them. On the whole, people like a president or an emperor may have great power but tend to be ignorant about ordinary people. 'He tends his flock like a shepherd: He gathers the lambs in his arms and carries them close to his heart.' What's Isaiah saying? This God who is more glorious than the most powerful of emperors also has a tender love for you.

The most tender of shepherds

'He gently leads those that have young.' A shepherd has to be considerate for those ewes with young, for the sake of the ewe's health and for the sake of the lamb's health. Isaiah applies that to God. It may be for those of you that do have young, the labour was painless, your children from day one slept every night, smiled every day and when they came to teenage years, they woke up the next morning, radiant in young adulthood. On the other hand it may be that for some, parenthood has brought a shock with it. All this new responsibility: you get home, look at the baby and say, 'We're to look after it? What do we do now?' In those circumstances – not for all, but for some – it's quite a shock. Sometimes those with young can feel as if they're like a hamster on its wheel. When their highest ambition in life is survival, some can feel as if God must surely disapprove of them, surely they should be out seeing the world converted before their next birthday, instead of counting off the hours until they can go to bed. Sometimes it's between the individual and God, and sometimes it's the way a church works, that someone who is struggling to cope with the demands of life, can feel as if 'God must surely disapprove of me because surely God wants me to be Super-parent!' Hear the Scriptures, and if this isn't your circumstance of life, hear it for others – 'He gently leads those that have young.' What are the signs of spiritual hard times in our society? How does the image of God as tender shepherd speak to you and speak through you? If this is what God is like, how must I relate to others that they sense in me the tenderness of God?

The God beyond compare

The chapter moves on again to the God beyond compare (verses 12-26). He is vast beyond creation (verse 12). It's partly a picture of a child playing with water, partly a picture of an architect in the ancient world, measuring off a building with a span of the hand and saying God is the celestial architect. When you sense the immensity and the grandeur of creation, recognise that that which is beyond our understanding is the gift of the creativity of God. He's vast beyond the human mind (verses 13,14). We can't teach God a thing or two. Here we understand both the necessity of revelation – this is a God beyond our understanding, Who must reveal Himself – but we also need to understand one of Paul's favourite words, 'mystery'. If this is a God beyond our understanding, we can never say, 'I've got God so sorted out that if you disagree with me, you must be wrong!' He reveals himself and we need his revelation. But he reveals himself as being beyond us so we never dare say, 'I've got God taped.'

Enduring beyond the nations

There are times when nations on the face of the earth have an awesome power. When the Americans went into Afghanistan, many said, is this a new Vietnam? But their technology was awesomely superior. We see the power of the powerful but God is enduring beyond the nations. If you visit the city of Rome you see something of the pride of nations. The most powerful empire of its day, left just with ruins. You see glorious buildings from the renaissance, a time when Rome was towering in the arts; and yet that moment was spent. It shouldn't be difficult for us from Britain to understand that the days of the glory of a nation are temporary. Britain is not as powerful as it used to be in the world. And I hope instead of craving the days of empire, we say, 'Empires come and go. But God endures for ever.' He endures beyond the nations.

He's incomparable with idols

Frequently Isaiah takes Israel to task for being tempted to assume that the gods of others should be their gods: that they might find a security that lasts in the gods of this world (verses 18-20). Most of us have gone beyond putting our trust in inanimate objects but there are other idols. Some rearrange their offices or their homes in line with Feng Shui; others say, 'My future is secure. I've got a pension in the stock market.' Isaiah says, 'Understand this ... your God is incomparable with any other source of security.'

He makes the mighty miniscule

I can never understand why anyone wants to take part in *Big Brother*. It seems to me that, increasingly with each series, it diminishes those who take part because they are exploited to an extraordinary degree. Isaiah says, 'God makes the mighty miniscule'(verses 21-24). God doesn't make a mockery of ordinary people in ordinary vulnerability. But where people take upon themselves the pride of power, God makes them miniscule. Isaiah says, princes are brought to nothing. It doesn't matter who we are; mortality is inescapable. The people are like grass and are blown away.

This God beyond compare

Isaiah moves back from the powerful people to the stars in the heavens (verses 25,26). He says again, there are none who can compare with God. The Babylonians were very keen on astrology. So some of the Jews would begin to think, 'Maybe we should get into astrology as well.' Isaiah says, 'Don't take astrology seriously. Don't read your charts just in case, don't think that there are powers in such things, your God is beyond compare.'

The Shepherd of the stars

He brings together these two strands of the magnificence of God and the intensely personal love of God when he speaks of the stars and says, He not only created them all but He calls them each by name (verse 26). This a picture of the stars coming out at night, as if God is the celestial conductor, in His authority over creation beckoning the stars, and out they come. It's poetry that speaks of the intense personal love of God because if God knows the stars by name, He's so much bigger than us! But if God calls the stars by name, how much more, being made in His image, does He call you by name? Does He know your needs and circumstances? Does He want to engage in love with you? He's transcendent but He's involved. He's intensely personal.

The Jews of this time were tempted to diminish God and Isaiah said, 'Let Him out of the box!' Are there times when we might put God into a box? A Sunday God; only on Sundays? A religious God, not interested in the rest of life? Not according to the Scriptures. A safe God, Who's ever so nice? A God for people 'like us'? I came across one church where the first time someone took the offering wearing a leather jacket, the deacons met together to agonise over whether the offering might have been tainted. How absurd we are. How easily we confuse the fads of human fashion with the eternal priorities of God.

Escape from defeatism

'I feel forgotten'

Then we move just briefly to the third theme. Isaiah who understands the infinite majesty and the intensely personal love of God, also understands the human response. Isaiah understands that some people, when they hear of God's grandeur, are likely to respond by saying:

'My way is hidden from the Lord; my cause is disregarded by my God.'
I feel neglected. There are times when it's not easy to see the way forward. There are times when we're faced with a problem and we pray and it's resolved and there are times when it seems that we are left to walk a hard journey with God. There are times when we might say, 'I feel forgotten by God.'

'We grow weary' (verse 30)

The promise comes – He renews us as we wait upon Him (verse 31). As we wait upon Him, hope in Him, put our trust in Him, lean on Him with all our weight. This is an active waiting upon God. There are times when we are so full of what's wrong, we don't have any space left to receive from God. We're so caught up in declaring the problem that we can't be in that place of responding to the goodness of God. There was a very simple way of praying that I was once taught by Richard Foster, called the hands down, hands up way of praying. He says sometimes he feels so full of the burdens in his life that he prays with his palms facing down and as he names those things that weigh upon his life, it's as if he was letting go of them into the hands of God. Only when he's released those things to God, not pretending they're not there but saying, 'God, I need you to be my burden bearer,' then he feels able to turn his hands the other way and say 'Lord, as you bear my burdens, grant me your peace.' Those that wait on the Lord will renew their strength. Glorious promise – you can escape from that sense of neglect, that sense of weariness, if you will come back to the resources of God.

Notice the Scripture doesn't say, you will renew your strength and be able to spend the rest of your Christian days like a hamster on a wheel. I've met churches that not only have a prayer meeting, they have a prayer meeting for the prayer meeting and some churches where, in order to get ready for the prayer meeting for the prayer meeting, you better pray on your own before the prayer meeting for the prayer meeting. I have a feeling that we may have missed the point; we are so busy in church activities we've forgotten how to be human. Maybe we need to say in our churches: Is this meeting really worth having? Maybe we need to say to people, if you have a hobby you would love to pursue, you don't need to repent of it. Maybe we need to see ourselves more as God's missionary people, released out into the local community to engage in those activities with God, that we are gifted to engage in. Maybe if Christians went to less church meetings and got involved in more hobbies, we'd have more things to talk about. Because if the only thing we have to talk about is church, and sometimes what's wrong with church, we haven't got an awful lot to say to those who don't go. Maybe we need to ask the question: Have we become a little too religious, a little too boring? If God wanted us to be doing church things all the time, He wouldn't have bothered with creating the cosmos. He'd have just made one gigantic cathedral and stuck us all in it! God has given us life in all its fullness. Jesus calls his followers to express the abundant life that is ours in Christ, that as we live abundantly, the majesty of God might somehow be glimpsed among us. Sometimes I fear we look more like the Pharisees than Jesus.

We will renew our strength

The final promise comes: '… those who hope in the Lord will renew their strength. They will soar on wings like eagles; they will run and not grow weary, they will walk and not be faint.' This verse had me puzzled when I first read it because it seemed as if it was round the wrong way. As a picture of the favour of God coming upon the people of God, it seemed to me as if you ought to start off walking and then start running and once you're running fast enough then, you can fly – that seemed just to be a logical progression. This is the reverse. You will fly, you will run, you will walk. What does that mean? Does that mean we get worn out, a little slower with time? Fly, run, walk – does that mean you start off well but you get slower with time? I think Isaiah is saying, there will be moments of soaring like an eagle; mountain top moments with God, but we're not meant to stay there. They're meant to inspire us to get on with living for Jesus. What's the running? I think it might be moments of intense activity, unsustainable intensity. You can do it for a while, but if you keep on like that, you're going to die very young. I think the walking isn't here meant to be second best; that's meant to be this. The strength of God comes not only for the mountain top experience, not only for the season of intense spiritual activity but for the ordinariness of life, that we might know God in the ordinary things.

There is a profound wisdom in these words of Isaiah. The mountain top moments are privileges for which we're grateful. The seasons of intense activity are moments of serving God that we may cherish for ever, but the same God comes in to the ordinary things of life. We are invited to know the grandeur of God in the checkout queue; to know the intensely personal love of God in the motorway queue; to know God's strength renewing us when we feel like our batteries have worn out. God wants to meet with you in your everyday. Here is your King. Isaiah doesn't solve the people's problems, the problems are still there. But he offers a new perspective. The problems were bigger than the Jews but Isaiah says, your God is bigger than your problems and so he speaks to them of the grandeur of God. He speaks to them of the intensely personal love of God who calls them by name like a shepherd and he says to them, 'You can move from weariness to God's strength, not only soaring like an eagle but in your everyday.'

Here is your God.

Keswick 2001 Tapes, Videos, CDs and Books

Catalogues and price lists of audio tapes of the Keswick Convention platform and seminar ministry, including much that is not included in this book, can be obtained from:

ICC
Silverdale Road
Eastbourne
BN20 7AB
Tel: 01323 643341
Fax: 01323 649240
www.icc.org.uk

Details of videos and CDs of selected sessions can also be obtained from the above address.

Some previous annual Keswick volumes (all published by STL/Authentic Media) can be obtained from:

The Keswick Convention Centre, Skiddaw Street, Keswick, Cumbria, CA12 4BY
Or from your local Christian Bookseller or direct from the publishers, Authentic Media, PO Box 300, Kingstown Broadway, Carlisle, Cumbria CA3 0QS, UK

Keswick 2003

The annual Keswick Convention takes place in the heart of the English Lake District, an area of outstanding natural beauty. It offers an unparalleled opportunity for listening to gifted Bible exposition, experiencing fellowship with Christians from all over the world and enjoying the grandeur of God's creation. Each of the weeks has a series of morning Bible readings, and then a varied programme of seminars and other events throughout the day, with evening meetings that combine worship and teaching. There is also a full programme for children and youth, and a special track for those with learning difficulties will take place in week 2. There is an interactive track aimed at those in their 20s and 30s, K2, which also takes place in week 2.

Speakers confirmed for the 2003 event are:
Bible Readings: Joe Stowell of the Moody Bible Institute, week 1; Charles Price of the People's Church, Toronto, week 2; Vaughan Roberts of St Ebbe's church, Oxford, week 3. Other speakers that have been confirmed so far include: Ann and Martin Allen, Steve Brady, Steve Chalke, Angus MacLeay, Jonathan Lamb, Peter Maiden and Terry Virgo.

For further information, please contact:

The Administrator
The Convention Office
PO Box 105
Uckfield
East Sussex
TN22 5GY
Tel: 01435 866034
email: office@keswickconv.com
Website: www.keswickconv.com